P9- EJO -931

ALEXANDER MACKENZIE

ALEXANDER MACKENZIE

FROM CANADA BY LAND

Ainslie Manson

A GROUNDWOOD BOOK
DOUGLAS & McINTYRE
TORONTO VANCOUVER BERKELEY

For Gavin Kertland Manson

Text copyright © 2003 Ainslie Manson

Groundwood Books / Douglas & McIntyre
720 Bathurst Street, Suite 500, Toronto, Ontario

We acknowledge for their financial support of our publishing program the
Canada Council for the Arts, the Ontario Arts Council, the Government
of Ontario through the Ontario Media Development Corporation's
Ontario Book Initiative and the Government of Canada through the Book
Publishing Industry Development Program (BPIDP).

ONTARIO ARTS COUNCIL
CONSEIL DES ARTS DE L'ONTARIO

National Library of Canada Cataloging in Publication
Manson, Ainslie
Alexander Mackenzie: from Canada by land / Ainslie Manson
ISBN 0-88899-483-4
1. Mackenzie, Alexander, Sir–Juvenile literature. 2. Northwest,
Canadian–Discovery and exploration–Juvenile literature. 3.
Explorers–Canada–Biography–Juvenile literature. 4. Fur
traders–Canada–Biography–Juvenile literature. I. Title.

FC3212.1.M46M363 2002   971.2'01'092   C2002-904617-3

Book design by Michael Solomon
Printed and bound in Canada

Contents

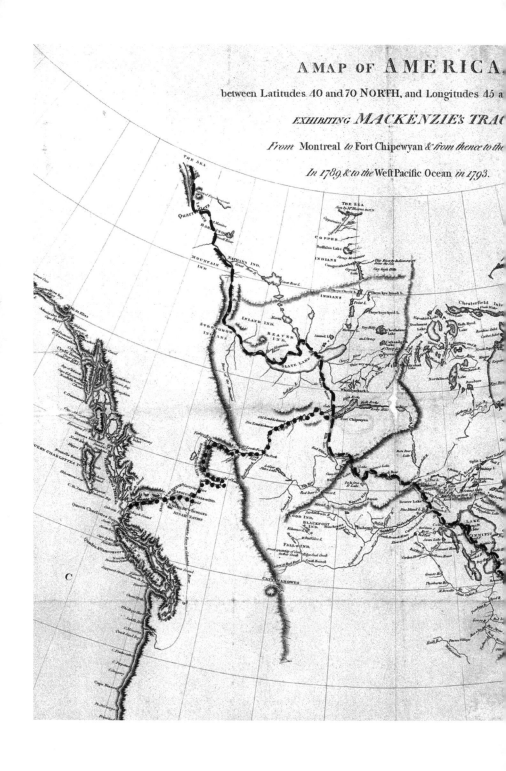

A MAP OF AMERICA

between Latitudes 40 and 70 NORTH, and Longitudes 45 a

EXHIBITING MACKENZIE's TRA

From Montreal to Fort Chipewyan & from thence to the

In 1789, & to the West Pacific Ocean in 1793.

Overleaf: A map from Mackenzie's *Voyages*, published in 1801. Dotted lines have been added to highlight Mackenzie's expeditions to the Northern Sea in 1789 and the Pacific Ocean in 1793.

1789 ▸-- -⁀

1793 ⁱ•·•·•···•⁰

PROLOGUE
July 22, 1793

"**D**o you plan to remain here to be sacrificed?" The trembling voice was barely audible.

Alexander Mackenzie tried to ignore the terrified voyageur tugging at his coattail. He was well aware of the canoes gliding silently toward them through the early morning haze. He was worried, too, but he wasn't going to show it.

He took a deep breath. "Pack our belongings into the canoes," he told his men, his voice steady. "I won't be long."

They were on a desolate section of Pacific coastline. They had run rapids, conquered mountains and fought forests thick with underbrush to reach this destination. Mackenzie refused to set off on the long journey home without determining their exact location.

He gazed at the sky instead of the sea, grateful that the clouds had cleared. Then he unpacked his surveying instruments. He did not turn around when he heard the scraping of the canoes landing on the pebble beach. He kept on with his work, but he secretly dreaded what might happen next.

This portrait of Alexander Mackenzie was painted in England, in 1801, by Court Painter Sir Thomas Lawrence.

One of his guides foamed at the mouth, he was so panic-stricken. "Any moment now they will start shooting their arrows and hurling their spears!" he whispered fiercely.

Mackenzie could feel his heart hammering in his chest. He knew he had to hurry but, emphasizing each word, he responded, "I cannot and will not leave until these calculations are completed. And I repeat, I will not be long."

But the newcomers simply surrounded Mackenzie and watched him work. When his job was finished, he proceeded with one final task. He mixed vermilion with grease, producing a red paint-like mixture, and in large, bold letters he wrote on a smooth rock face:

Alexander Mackenzie, from Canada by land, the twenty-second of July, one thousand seven hundred and ninety-three.

As he stepped into his canoe, Mackenzie was acutely aware that he was not welcome here. He had often imagined the culmination of this journey, but he had imagined it as a joyous time. Instead, he and his companions were desperate to depart. They turned their backs on the Pacific. This was no time for celebration.

The native people watched silently as the white men left. They were in no mood for celebration either. They hoped the interlopers were truly leaving. Why had they come here? Who were they? And what did they want?

CHAPTER ONE
Stornoway, Scotland

O UT OF SIGHT, but close to all the action, twelve-year-old Alexander Mackenzie sat at the end of one of Stornoway's busy wharves. He wrapped his arms around his legs and tried to digest his father's words.

"Alexander, we'll be leaving Stornoway," Kenneth Mackenzie had said that morning at breakfast. "We're going to America."

Alexander and his family had had nothing but unhappiness over the last few years, but it was hard to imagine leaving. Stornoway was home. Alexander gazed at the ships swinging at anchor with the incoming tide. His mind was in turmoil. On the one hand, he already felt the dreadful ache of homesickness but, on the other, what an adventure it would be to sail out through the narrows on one of those fine ships!

All his life Alexander had lived on the windswept Isle of Lewis, in the Hebrides, off the west coast of Scotland. He had been born in his grandparents' house in the village and then, at a very young age, he had moved with his family to Melbost Farm.

Stornoway was a fishing village, with a population of

fewer than one thousand people. Even though it was small, fishermen from all around the world knew about its excellent natural harbor. It was also a renowned recruiting ground for the Hudson's Bay Company, the oldest fur-trading company in North America. Men raised in the Hebrides adapted well to the severe climate in North America and the hardships of a fur trader's life.

Alexander knew many Lewismen who had gone to the New World and become involved in the fur trade. Their lives sounded fascinating. He thought it would be wonderful to explore an unknown land and to paddle canoes down fast-flowing rivers.

For several generations the Mackenzies had been involved in the military and, compared to many on Lewis, they were reasonably well off. Soldiers were on constant call to fight for clan and country but, in return, each was granted a tack, or parcel of land, for which they paid only a nominal fee.

Melbost Farm was Kenneth Mackenzie's tack, and Alexander's early years there were happy. He had two younger sisters, Sybilla and Margaret, and an older brother, Murdoch, with whom he shared a great love of adventure and a longing to go to sea. His friends were the sons of fishermen and sailors. The boys rowed, fished and sailed in all kinds of weather.

Alexander also liked to visit the harbor with his friends. There were so many ships coming and going, so many different people setting off on voyages. The boys listened to stories told by soldiers, fishermen and fur traders.

In the fur trade, men traveled to places no white man had ever been before, places where only native people lived. The land was their home and they had lived there for thousands of years. There were many different tribes and they spoke many different languages.

The boys also learned about the unusual animals of that faraway land. There were bears, moose, buffalos and beavers. Alexander tried to imagine what beavers actually looked like, with teeth so sharp they could cut down trees and large, flat tails. Although beavers were small, they were plentiful, and it was because of their valuable fur coats that a whole new continent beyond the sea was opening up. Beaver hats had became the fashion in Europe, and the best beaver pelts came from the harsh Canadian north.

The new land was indeed a land of adventure and opportunity. It seemed that there a man could do just about whatever job he pleased to earn his living.

Alexander was aware of the changes taking place on Lewis and all over Scotland. The rights of the tacksmen had practically been removed, and the nominal fee that his father had once paid for his tack had risen higher and higher. It was now almost impossible for Kenneth Mackenzie to afford the increases.

The Mackenzies were not alone in these difficulties. The economy of the island was at an all-time low. Islanders were unable to produce enough food even for their own families. Each month Alexander saw more and more of his friends and relations leaving.

Melbost Farm was a sizable piece of land. Kenneth Mackenzie had always hoped he could pass it on to his eldest son, Murdoch. But with the changes, the land was no longer his to pass on, and so Murdoch chose a different career. Because of his love of the sea, he became a ship's surgeon.

Alexander missed his brother terribly. Everything at home seemed different. Not only had Murdoch left a huge void, but he and his sisters shared few of the same interests. His father was constantly distracted and then his mother became ill.

In the months that followed, his mother died and news arrived that Murdoch had been drowned in a shipwreck off Canada's Atlantic coast. These family tragedies influenced the Mackenzies in their final decision to leave the island.

In 1774, following the example of so many other Lewis families, Kenneth Mackenzie decided to emigrate to America. He sailed first, to prepare the way. He had a brother in New York who was a successful merchant, and so New York became his destination.

Alexander Mackenzie was born in his grandparents' home in Stornoway on the Isle of Lewis.

CHAPTER TWO
Off to the New World

Ⅰ N NOVEMBER, 1774, Alexander waved goodbye to
Lewis from the deck of the *Peace & Plenty*. Though the
ship's name seemed a good omen, his emotions were
mixed. He told himself the tears in his eyes were from
the wind, but he stayed on deck, looking back, until he
could no longer see the island that had been his home.
He was accompanied only by two maiden aunts. His sisters were left behind in the care of his mother's family.
He had no idea when he would see them again.

Alexander had hardly set foot on American soil before
the War of Independence began. Some American colonists
wanted independence from Great Britain. Others, like
Alexander's father and uncle, wished to remain loyal to
their mother country. They joined the King's Royal
Regiment of New York as lieutenants. Almost immediately, the Royal Yorks, as they were more often called, left for
the front. Alexander stayed behind with his aunts.

He started school amid the revolutionary turmoil of
New York City. Troops were gathering, and battles
between the Redcoats (the British) and the Rebels were
breaking out even within the city limits.

An engraving shows New York harbor as it looked at the time of Alexander Mackenzie's arrival.

Alexander's aunts felt responsible for their young nephew's safety. They decided they would be safer in the upper part of New York state, where they had family connections.

And so they moved to the Mohawk Valley, and at first it did seem a peaceful spot. But soon the war was upon them there as well. A fierce battle was fought on the nearby Mohawk River.

By this time Loyalists were fleeing the American colonies by the thousands, crossing the border into Canada. At fifteen, Alexander was sent to the safe haven of Montreal, his third move in three years. He was now separated from all of his family, but fortunately the people his aunts had arranged for him to live with were kind and hospitable.

Alexander liked Montreal. It was an exciting city with an interesting past. The original stone buildings had been built by French fur traders and settlers. They had been surrounded by high protective stone walls. The walls were crumbling away now, but they had once been built to guard against Iroquois attacks.

When he wasn't in school, Alexander explored the narrow cobbled streets. He listened with interest to the different languages – he heard French, different native dialects as well as the familiar accents of many Scots.

Outside the old walls, new wooden buildings were under construction. Beyond these buildings, and beyond the tilled fields, there was nothing but forest – endless forest that stretched right across the continent to the unknown west coast.

Alexander could see that most of Montreal's four thousand inhabitants were either involved in the military, like his father and uncle, or they were part of the fur trade.

In the harbor, he recognized many ships that had

Those loyal to the British fled to Canada at the time of the American Revolution.

visited Stornoway. Seeing them with their sails furled, being loaded and unloaded, rekindled his fascination with the fur trade. He decided that this industry would give him a chance to travel and explore. Canada was no longer a dream on the other side of the ocean. And so he left school to pursue his chosen career.

Chapter Three
Montreal

A T   T H E   A G E of seventeen, Alexander Mackenzie
joined Finlay, Gregory & Company, a small firm of
fur merchants and traders. He began as a clerk in the
counting house, where detailed records were kept for the
Montreal headquarters and the interior posts.

Young Mackenzie's work involved writing letters and
filling out order forms. He had to keep track of the number
and types of pelts received, the credit owed to the
native people, and provisions needed to supply each
voyageur for the season. The company gave the
voyageurs everything they required except their paddles.
Paddles were considered personal belongings, like the
colorful sashes the men wore, which had been woven by
their wives and sweethearts.

Mackenzie did not spend all of his time in the office.
He also ran messages and visited the warehouses. He was
required to learn enough French so that he could converse
easily with voyageurs and traders alike.

His duties were varied because the work was so seasonal.
From the start James Finlay, the senior partner, was
aware of his young employee's energy and enthusiasm

and gave him a chance to try his hand at every job. Mackenzie discovered that the fur-trading business was complex, and the trade turn-around time was long and complicated. He explained this process in his journal:

> The agents are obliged to order the necessary goods from England in the month of October, eighteen months before they can leave Montreal; that is, they are not shipped from London until the spring following, when they arrive in Canada in the summer. In the course of the following winter they are made up into such articles as are required for the savages; they are then packed into parcels of ninety pounds so that they do not get to market until the ensuing winter, when they are exchanged for furs, which come to Montreal the next fall, and from thence are shipped, chiefly to London, where they are not sold or paid for before the succeeding spring... which is forty-two months after the goods were ordered in Canada.

In the autumn, when the trees turned brilliant red and gold, Alexander watched with interest as the fur traders and voyageurs returned to the city from their distant posts. Although the fur traders negotiated trades, the voyageurs were hired hands. They were simply responsible for the transport of furs and of trading goods between the St. Lawrence Valley and the Northwest. A voyageur's salary for six months was about three times more than a farm worker earned in a year.

In the fall, though the air was clear and frosty outside, it was far from fresh in the warehouses. Mackenzie tried to ignore the sour stench that grew worse and worse as

In the Montreal harbor, Mackenzie recognized many of the same ships he had seen in Stornoway on the Isle of Lewis.

the season progressed and the bales of dried, untanned pelts grew higher and higher.

There were all kinds of pelts: bear, buffalo, deer, elk, fisher, fox, lynx, marten, mink, muskrat, otter, raccoon, weasel, wolf and wolverine. But the most prized pelts of all were beaver.

When winter came to Montreal, it was bitterly cold. But Mackenzie discovered there was an advantage to the freezing weather – as the temperature dropped, the stench in the warehouses became far more tolerable!

He had never before seen so much snow and ice. Sometimes he would stop on his way to or from the warehouse and stare in amazement at the few ships that had not left the harbor in time. They would be locked in ice until spring. The mighty St. Lawrence River was frozen all the way to Quebec City and beyond.

During the winter Alexander helped supervise the unpacking and rebaling of all the trading goods that had arrived on ships during the previous summer.

As he explained in the preface to his journal, these were the goods that the native people would receive in exchange for furs:

> The articles necessary for this trade are coarse woollen cloths of different kinds; milled blankets of different sizes; arms and ammunition; twist and carrot tobacco; Manchester goods; linens, and coarse sheetings; thread, lines and twine; common hardware; cutlery and iron-mongery of several descriptions; kettles of brass and copper, and sheet iron; silk and cotton handkerchiefs; hats, shoes and hose; calicoes and printed cottons, &c. &c. &c. Spirituous liquors and provisions are purchased in Canada.

Everything had to be repacked in 88-pound (40-kg) bales or "pieces" that could be handled easily in canoes or carried on portages.

There were few visitors to the city in the wintertime but, with many of the traders at home until spring, it was a social season. There were many parties with music and dancing.

Winter was also a time when an occasional lull at work gave Mackenzie time to question James Finlay about his experiences in the *pays d'en haut*. He had been the first trader to travel as far west as the Saskatchewan Valley. He had wintered there even before Alexander was

Native people traded their furs for firearms.

born. The older man spoke in such detail of his adventures that Mackenzie could almost see the wolves on the snow-covered lakes and the dark, silent forests stretching on for miles.

When the snow and ice melted in the early spring, Mackenzie's duties changed again. Now he helped to organize the transportation of the traded goods to Lachine, 29 miles (13 km) upriver from Montreal above the treacherous rapids. Once in Lachine the goods were stored in temporary shelters until the ice broke up. There was much guessing and betting as to exactly which day this would be. When the ice moved, so did the canoe brigades.

The echoes of the voyageurs' songs had no sooner

"CONTINENTAL"
COCKED HAT.
(1776)

"NAVY"
COCKED HAT.
(1800)

ARMY. (1837)

CLERICAL.
(Eighteenth Century)

(THE WELLINGTON.)
(1812)

CIVIL.

(THE PARIS BEAU.)
(1815)

(THE D'ORSAY.)
(1820)

(THE REGENT.)
(1825)

MODIFICATIONS OF THE BEAVER HAT.

The popularity of fashionable hats for gentlemen in Europe fueled the fur trade in the New World.

faded in the distance than the tall ships would arrive from England. They came loaded with more trading goods and the cycle began again.

Several years went by. Mackenzie's work was not always stimulating and the hours were sometimes long, but each season he learned and understood more.

The first phase of Mackenzie's apprenticeship came to

an end in the spring of 1783. Finlay, Gregory & Company then put him in charge of a consignment of trading goods and sent him off to tend their post in Detroit.

CHAPTER FOUR
Fort Detroit

B EFORE leaving Lachine in 1783, Mackenzie and his voyageurs attended the annual dockside feast. There they drank glasses of precious Madeira wine and enjoyed bear meat, venison, sturgeon and fine cheeses as they said their goodbyes to friends and family.

Mackenzie eagerly climbed into his canoe. The adventure he had been waiting for was about to begin. He seated himself in the customary manner just behind the middle seats. This was a large *canot de maître*, a freight canoe, and it could hold up to four tons including fourteen men. Shouts of "bon voyage!" sounded across the water as the canoes pulled away from the dock.

Each voyageur in the canoe performed a different job. The *avant* sat in the bow and acted as guide. His job was to watch the waters ahead for rocks and debris. The *gouvernail* sat in the stern and guided the canoe based on the directions given by the *avant*. The others were the *milieux*. They sat in pairs in the middle of the canoe and did the paddling.

Mackenzie at this stage of his career was still a clerk. He would not be considered a bourgeois, a man of higher

Songs of the Voyageurs

The voyageurs had a song for every mood and occasion. If someone was sluggish as they set off in the morning they would perhaps try a rousing chorus of "Frère Jacques." Or they sang the paddling song "Send Her Along" as they dreamed of returning in autumn to their loved ones:

> *Envoyons de l'avant, nos gens!*
> *Envoyons de l'avant!*
> *Envoyons de l'avant, nos gens!*
> *Envoyons de l'avant!*
> *Quand on part de chantier,*
> *Mes chers amis, tous le coeur gai,*
> *Pour aller voir tous nos parents,*
> *Mes chers amis, le coeur content.*

One of the saddest songs and one of the only songs with a Canadian origin was "Petit Rocher." It tells the legend of Cadieux, an early eighteenth-century fur trader. Cadieux returned to his camp one night to find it surrounded by a band of dangerous Iroquois. He helped his wife and children escape to safety on the river, and then had to hide in the bush. Eventually he was found in a shallow grave that he had dug himself. Beside him, written on birchbark with his own blood, were the words to the song.

> *Oh, little rock, on the mountain so mighty,*
> *Here have I come at the end of the fighting.*
> *Ye gentle echoes, oh hear my painful breathing,*
> *As here I languish, awaiting my death.*

Voyageurs rest at the end of a long day.

social standing, until he became a partner in the company. But still, the company clerks were rarely allowed to paddle. There were many such rules and regulations in the fur trade. Mackenzie quickly saw, however, that he would never have had the strength to paddle for hours like these voyageurs.

Most of the voyageurs were French Canadians from farms in the St. Lawrence Valley. They were strong, powerful men even though they were not tall. No man taller than five feet five inches (165 cm) was hired as a voyageur, because the canoes were simply not large enough. Mackenzie towered over these men. He noted the massive shoulders of the two voyageurs paddling in front of him. They could average fifty strokes a minute, hour after hour!

The life of a voyageur was not all song and laughter. Most grew old before their time because of the grueling long days and the heavy lifting that their work involved. Over the years to come Mackenzie would see many small crosses along the routes traveled by the voyageurs. They marked the resting places of men who had drowned or died from injuries or disease during their travels.

The native people rarely paddled either. They were hired as interpreters, hunters and guides. Often in their role as hunters, they would walk along the shore for hours in search of that night's dinner.

Many canoes set out together from Lachine that morning, but most soon waved their farewells. They were headed to Grand Portage and would follow the Ottawa River.

Mackenzie's canoe followed the St. Lawrence to Lake Ontario, then paddled along the shore of Lake Erie to reach Detroit. There were several lengthy portages along the way, but fortunately the paths through the dense forest in this region were well trodden.

At every portage the canoe had to be unloaded and reloaded from the water. The voyageurs would jump overboard before the bottom of the canoe could scrape against the lake floor. Boxes and bundles *and* bourgeois all had to be carried ashore.

The birchbark canoe was amazingly strong, but still had to be handled with great care. Packing up was an art. No pointed box corner could be allowed to dig into the delicate hull. All boxes and bundles had to rest on the staves.

In the days that followed, Mackenzie and the voyageurs rose each morning before dawn and paddled at least four hours before breakfast. For their midday meal they simply chewed on a piece of pemmican as they paddled.

They were on the water fourteen to seventeen hours a day, and Mackenzie was often tired and cramped long before they made camp at sundown (and long before the paddlers themselves were tired!). By the time they dug into their evening meal, everyone was famished. Table manners were forgotten as some ate from cups, some from their hats, and others from indents in the rocks. If they had no utensils, the men lapped up their food.

On these journeys the menu often included great chunks of fatty pork, which is why these French Canadian voyageurs were nicknamed *mangeurs du lard*. They were also sometimes called "Goers and Comers" because they would go out from Montreal every spring and come back in the fall.

At each portage the canoes had to be unloaded and reloaded. Between Montreal and Lake Huron there were thirty carrying places or portages. It often took the voyageurs two to three months to complete this part of the journey.

Mackenzie was puzzled at first by the hourly stops the men made to light their pipes. But he soon realized that the smoke helped to keep the hordes of mosquitoes and blackflies away. Some voyageurs, he had heard, made a bug repellent of bear grease and skunk oil. Smoke definitely seemed preferable! Also, distances were measured in "pipes." Allowing for a variance in wind and current, *trois pipes* was generally about 70 miles (32 km).

The men often sang as they traveled. One paddler in each canoe was actually paid extra for his ability to lead the group in song and keep the beat. The songs helped to keep up morale and kept the men paddling in unison. Many of the songs Mackenzie learned on that first journey were folk songs that had come to Canada from France during the 1700s.

Mackenzie slept in a tent, but the voyageurs slept under their canoes. Their journey to Detroit took several weeks.

Detroit was at the heart of rich fur-trading country, and it had been an important center for many years. In the early days, under French control, the post had been called Fort Pontchartrain. Now under English control, the whole area including the fort and the town was called Detroit. The name had come from the French, Ville d'Etroit (city of the strait).

Detroit was a smaller town than Montreal, but that did not mean that Mackenzie's job was easier. He was in charge now, and he saw immediately that the post had problems.

His first duties were those of a diplomat because the native people and the traders were not compatible. Their relationships had to improve before the post could run smoothly. Mackenzie conscientiously studied the customs of the native people and systematically questioned the trappers and traders. He helped them to understand one another better, gaining the confidence of all who worked for him. He took command and made his own decisions and the post soon thrived.

The Montreal traders ("free traders," such as those who worked for Finlay, Gregory & Company) had an advantage over those who were employed by the Hudson's Bay Company. They could bargain with the native people, choosing their own trading goods when they determined what the local natives wanted.

Usually they entertained the native people before the bargaining began with a feast known as a regale. They would hand around food, tobacco and watered-down rum. The number of pelts from the Detroit area must have increased significantly, because at the end of that first year, Normand McLeod made the long trip to Detroit to tell twenty-two-year-old Mackenzie how pleased the firm was with his progress.

James Finlay had retired and Normand McLeod was a senior partner. The firm, now known as Gregory, McLeod & Company, showed Alexander Mackenzie their appreciation by asking him to become a partner, too. This meant he would own shares in the company and he would have a voice and a vote at all meetings. The offer was a true stamp of approval and a great honor. He accepted without hesitation. Alexander Mackenzie was now considered a bourgeois.

Mackenzie's hard work had paid off in his short time at Fort Detroit, but his firm knew that their trading days in that area were numbered. The American Revolution was now over. The newly determined border was still unclear, but it was quite certain that Detroit, by treaty, would now be within the territory of the United States.

Because of this, the company was preparing to trade further to the north and west, in areas still entirely under British possession. Mackenzie's new partnership therefore held one condition. He would have to spend the following winter in the north country, the famous *pays d'en haut*. It was something he had been longing to do.

In 1784, Alexander wound up his business at Fort Detroit and immediately went to Grand Portage on Lake Superior, where the partners would make plans for the coming year.

CHAPTER FIVE
Grand Portage

FROM HIS first days in the fur trade, Mackenzie had heard tales of Grand Portage. Strategically situated between east and west, it was the summer meeting place for several different fur-trading companies. Most of the small companies that met here were now banded together in a partnership known as the North West Company, but there were independents as well, such as Gregory, McLeod.

At Grand Portage the company members exchanged pelts and trading goods, received news from home, held annual general meetings, hired men (and no doubt fired them) and made future plans.

As they neared the renowned center in the summer of 1784, the voyageurs with Mackenzie laughed and joked, and a few of them wondered aloud whether the pretty young women they had met the previous summer would still be at the fort.

A few miles from their destination the men made a brief stop. They wanted to look their best upon arrival, and so they washed, shaved and put on their cleanest clothes.

When they came within sight of the fort, the customary welcoming salute, the *feu de joie*, was fired from the stockade. The voyageurs answered the salute with one of their own. Clutching their paddles in front of them with both hands, they slammed them down on the gunnels and raised them up above their heads three times, cheering wildly.

Mackenzie could not believe the din when they landed at the busy jetty. The dock was sizable, but still they had difficulty finding space! Excitement filled the air. Grand Portage was like a small village for most of the year, but during these summer months its population doubled.

Dogs barked and languages melded as Scots, French Canadians and native people greeted one another. Mackenzie found the noise deafening. On the peaceful

VIEW of the GRAND PORTAGE on LAKE SUPERIOR.

There were several buildings within the walls of the fort at Grand Portage. The fort included all the "modern conveniences" of the day so that business would run smoothly and the proprietors and clerks would be comfortable during their visits.

journey from Fort Detroit there had only been the sound of dipping paddles and the voyageurs' songs.

But Mackenzie was quick to get into the spirit of fun in Grand Portage. This was his first social occasion in months. Grand Portage, he discovered, was everyone's favorite stop. It was not only a place of work, it was like a very large family reunion. The evening meal, for example, was a banquet for one and all, in the renowned Great Hall. He described it in his journal:

> The proprietors, clerks, guides, and interpreters, mess together, to the number of sometimes an hundred, at several tables, in one large hall, the provision consisting of bread, salt pork, beef, hams, fish, and venison, butter, peas, Native corn, potatoes, tea, spirits, wine, &c. and plenty of milk, for which purpose several milch cows are constantly kept.

Here at Grand Portage tobacco and rum were free. Too much drinking often led to arguments between the voyageurs from Montreal and those from the *pays d'en haut*. The two groups were constantly trying to convince one another of their superiority. When words failed to prove a point, fighting often followed, and many would end up in the "Common Gaol" as it was known.

As the night wore on and celebrations became uproarious, Mackenzie noticed more than a few men being escorted off to spend the night in the grotty lockup!

The *hommes du nord* had probably been born in or near Montreal, but these voyageurs rarely got back there and they seemed to have little in common with the *mangeurs du lard.* The *hommes du nord* traveled from the *pays d'en haut* to Grand Portage in the spring with their furs, then back to their northern posts with trading goods. They lived on fish, game, pemmican and wild rice.

The two groups even dressed differently, and they argued about whose clothing was the most practical. The *mangeurs du lard* wore wool shirts, handwoven sashes and red woolen caps made by their families. The *hommes du nord* wore buckskin shirts, leggings and moccasins made by the native people.

Mackenzie met several newcomers at his first company meeting. Peter Pangman and John Ross, both experienced traders, had recently joined Gregory, McLeod as partners. But Mackenzie's most pleasant surprise was meeting his cousin Roderick McKenzie for the first time. They were first cousins even though their names were spelled differently. Roderick had joined the company as a clerk on his recent arrival in Montreal. "Rory" and Alexander were the same age, and they quickly became close friends.

Alexander had lived without family for some time. His father had died before the end of the war. His sisters were still in Scotland and his two aunts in New York. Rory helped to fill a void and for the rest of their days the cousins' lives were closely interwoven.

CHAPTER SIX
The Pays d'en haut

NINE MILES (14 km) straight uphill. The grand portage was the start of Mackenzie's journey to the *pays d'en haut* in 1785. Known as one of the longest, most difficult "carrying places" in the country, it was a grueling journey.

"This is a labour which cattle cannot conveniently perform," said Mackenzie. "Both horses and oxen were tried by the company without success."

His voyageurs were now the *hommes du nord* – men who only journeyed back and forth between the north country and Grand Portage. Mackenzie had heard them boast of their strength, and he witnessed it now as they strained to carry more than their allotted two packs at a time, each 88 pounds (40 kg). If they could accomplish this feat, they would earn a bonus, and many of them did.

He was also introduced to a different type of canoe at the top of the portage – the *canot du nord*. This canoe was considerably smaller than the 36-foot (11-m) long *canot de maître*. It was navigated by only four to six men and was used in this territory because it was easier to handle in the swifter rivers. It was also easier to portage.

Mackenzie had grown up in the harsh climate of the Hebrides and he had been in North America for several years, but he had never encountered such severe weather as he now experienced. The ice and snow often came to stay in October and rarely left before May.

His post, or fort as he called it, was on Lac Ile à la Crosse. The lake and fort were named after the game of Lacrosse which was played there by the native people.

The luxury and sumptuous feasts of Grand Portage now seemed a dream. Mackenzie's trading post was like all the others in the area – a simple cluster of log cabins built where a couple of native trails converged. A few of the buildings had no windows; windows just let in more cold.

At Fort Detroit, Mackenzie had learned how to negotiate with the native people and how to deal diplomatically with the established traders. These skills now held him in good stead.

His partners at Gregory, McLeod & Company had instructed him to learn more about the surrounding countryside and expand the territory from which they could obtain furs. The main object was to make more money and Mackenzie liked this challenge. He was a businessman and he set to work with enthusiasm.

In Detroit most of his duties had been performed from behind a desk, but here he was usually out of doors. He traveled with trappers and hunters, not shooting or setting the traps himself, but showing interest, learning how each task was done and gaining the confidence of everyone he worked with.

For years Mackenzie had been aware that the native people were the backbone of the fur trade. Now he wit-

Canoes on the Churchill River, close to where Mackenzie spent his first winter in the *pays d'en haut.*

nessed this first hand. They knew the country inside out. They knew the rivers and the shortcuts to other posts and where to find mammals, birds and fish. They also knew how long the ice and snow would last and therefore, how much food had to be collected before winter set in. The leaves had already changed color when Mackenzie arrived at Lac Ile à la Crosse. He had to depend on the native people for his food supply.

Like all the bourgeois, Mackenzie generally stuck to his thick woolen clothing. But he, like many northern traders, must have found that the traditional clothing, made from animal skins, was far better at keeping a man from freezing to death when the temperatures dropped below zero.

The native people introduced Mackenzie to snowshoes. In all kinds of weather he could then trek back and forth to other posts. Most of these visits were for business purposes. It was a lonely existence.

That year Gregory, McLeod & Company had kept Roderick McKenzie in Grand Portage. But the following year Alexander was delighted to receive news that they were sending his cousin to the *pays d'en haut* as well. Rory was posted to Ile à la Crosse but his job would be to set up a new outpost at Lac-au-Serpent about 45 miles (75 km) to the east.

William McGillivray, a North West Company employee had also been requested to set up a post at Lac-

Au façon du nord

Several of the traders had "country wives" at Grand Portage or in the *pays d'en haut*, and William McGillivray was one of them. He and his wife Susan would no doubt have been married "*au façon du nord*" (in the northern way). In this ceremony the bride was given away to the trader by her father or a native leader, and then a special ritual followed. The bride was escorted to the fort where other native wives removed all her grease, paint and leather clothing and bathed her. The ceremony concluded when, after the bath, she was dressed in European-style clothing and brought to her husband.

McGillivray and Susan had twin sons, Simon and Joseph. Several years later when they were christened in Montreal, Mackenzie was made one of the godfathers. Only a few country wives went to eastern Canada or to England with their trader husbands once they had retired from the fur trade. But despite this, native leaders encouraged these marriages. The relationships seemed to help rather than hinder bonds between white men and the native people. And the children from these marriages were the beginning of Métis society.

Some people think that Mackenzie also had a country wife and two children during his years in Canada, but there are no written records to prove this.

au-Serpent. Though he and Roderick were in competition, they built their small trading cabins quite close to one another and became friends. Alexander frequently enjoyed visits from both of them.

William McGillivray and Alexander Mackenzie looked so similar that they were often mistaken for brothers. They both had red, curly hair and the same long, slender faces. They spoke with the same Scottish burr, too. Strangers quickly learned to tell the two men apart because Alexander Mackenzie had a deep dimple in his chin. He also had a set, determined mouth that indicated the obstinate side of his nature.

Gregory, McLeod & Company had ninety men working at its northern posts that year. The North West Company had two hundred and fifty men. Competition was strong, and McGillivray and the cousins often found they were trading with the same native people. But they were wise enough to realize that there was a great deal to be gained by cooperation.

Yet in many circumstances, the competing companies never learned to sort out their differences. On Lake Athabasca John Ross, an employee of Gregory, McLeod & Company, and Nor'Wester Peter Pond were in constant conflict.

Everyone in the fur trade knew of Peter Pond. His greatest desire was to find a route to the Pacific coast, build a trading post there, and trade with China and Russia. With this goal in mind, he was always on the move and he had traveled farther west than any other white man. He was fascinating to talk to, much admired, but definitely a loner and he was known for his violent temper.

A tepee and a trapper's cabin in the *pays d'en haut*.

Mackenzie had first heard Peter Pond's name in Detroit. Pond had started in the fur trade there. And he had left, Mackenzie was told, because he was suspected of killing a man in a duel.

Then many years later, in the *pays d'en haut*, Pond had been brought to trial for the murder of a fur trader. He had been acquitted, but suspicion hung over him like a dark cloud.

In the spring of 1787, when John Ross was shot in a scuffle at Pond's Athabascan post, Pond's name was associated with murder yet again. It was a sticky situation. Everyone agreed that Pond had a fiery temper, but was he capable of murder? Perhaps he was simply in the wrong places at the wrong times.

When news of Ross's death reached Grand Portage, Gregory, McLeod & Company and the North West

Company held an emergency meeting. The brutal rivalry had to be stopped. Joining the two companies seemed to be the solution.

The North West Company became a partnership of a number of small companies. It now increased its shares, allotting one each to John Gregory, Normand McLeod, Peter Pangman, and the youngest partner, Alexander Mackenzie.

Mackenzie was impressed by the size and complexity of the organization. "Consider the number of men employed in the concern," he wrote in the prologue of his journal, "fifty clerks, seventy-one interpreters and clerks, 1,120 canoe men and thirty-five guides."

But he was quick to note that Simon McTavish, McGillivray's uncle, appeared to hold the reins of the newly organized association. He was chief executive and his company, McTavish, Frobisher & Company, in effect managed the North West Company. Simon McTavish was bossy and arrogant. Not everyone found him easy to work with.

Mackenzie was wary of the older man and was wise enough to watch and observe his methods of management without voicing too many opinions of his own. But McTavish seemed to take an instant dislike to Mackenzie. Perhaps he felt threatened by the young trader. Perhaps the two Scots were too similar, both being hard working, ambitious and competitive.

CHAPTER SEVEN
Lake Athabasca

THE SHAREHOLDERS all agreed on one point. Changes had to be made at their Lake Athabasca post. Even before the shooting, the company had decided that Pond should retire the following year. He was forty-seven, which was considered old in the rigorous fur trade. They had been looking for a replacement. And now, though Pond had not been arrested, he would soon have to go to Montreal to stand trial. They decided that they needed an apprentice for Pond – someone who could work with him for one winter, someone who could learn from him and, at the same time, plan ahead and reorganize the post.

Mackenzie was chosen for the job. He was strong, courageous and twenty-five years younger than Pond. Several of the shareholders had observed him in leadership roles, and they spoke highly of his success both at Lac Ile à la Crosse and in Detroit. Even McTavish agreed that he had proved himself an excellent trader capable of tackling challenges. Though possibly he was simply seizing the opportunity to employ Mackenzie far away from Montreal headquarters!

Mackenzie was full of energy, and he was keen to see as much of the country as possible. But on the long trek back to Lac Ile à la Crosse and then on to Lake Athabasca, he must have wondered what it would be like to be shut up in a small cabin, in the depths of winter, with a possible murderer.

Peter Pond was a rough diamond, but he was a born explorer and a crafty trader. He had mapped large areas of the Athabascan region, and he had contributed a great deal of business to the company. Mackenzie knew he could learn a lot from him.

No doubt sensing Mackenzie's trust, and seeing his enthusiasm, Pond relaxed and took pleasure in his company. He knew Mackenzie would be taking over his post, and he willingly shared his experiences. A great deal of what he had to pass on was simply in his head, but tactfully and methodically Mackenzie asked questions and made notes.

Pond was full of ideas. Mackenzie was impressed that he was well on the way to solving one of the fur traders' greatest problems. This was the difficulty of carrying great canoe loads of food supplies not only from Montreal to Grand Portage, but to the more remote posts as well. Pond realized that pemmican was the answer, especially on long journeys. The native people Pond had met trusted him, and they had the main pemmican ingredient, buffalo, at their disposal. They would be pleased to act as suppliers. And the traders would find they had more room in the canoes for trading goods.

Many of the local native people had been trading with the Hudson's Bay Company posts on Hudson's Bay. By situating himself in this region, Peter Pond had suc-

Pemmican

Pemmican was a native food. The word comes from the Cree words *pimmi* (meat) and *kon* (fat).

It was made by pounding thin slices of dried meat (deer, elk or buffalo) between two stones until the fibers separated. The pounded meat was then sewn into a skin bag.

Most explorers, traders and voyageurs did not consider pemmican their favorite dish but "a little time reconciles it to the palate," Mackenzie claimed. It was a vital food on both his journeys.

Pemmican was nutritious and easily preserved, and it was a timesaver. The hours usually spent hunting and cooking could be used instead as travel time.

"There is another sort," Mackenzie wrote, "made with the addition of marrow and dried berries, which is of a superior quality." Or when time allowed, pemmican could be fried with a little more fat and some flour and served hot. This sticky mush was called "rubaboo."

The Earl of Southesk never got used to it. Traveling in the 1800s he wrote, "Take scrapings from the driest outside corner of a very stale piece of cold roast beef, add to it lumps of tallowy rancid fat, then garnish all with long human hairs, and short hairs of oxen and dogs, or both, and you have a fair imitation of common pemmican, though I should rather suppose it to be less nasty."

ceeded in luring many of them to his post, instead. This arrangement was far more convenient for them as the trek to and from the Bay took months. There was another advantage, too; the North West Company's traders were permitted to decide for themselves what their trading goods would be. Their shareholders didn't even worry too much about the amount of liquor that was being distributed. Unfortunately the three most valued and requested trading items were rum, guns and ammunition, and they did not mix well. Tobacco was another popular commodity.

Mackenzie noted Pond's techniques with interest. Now rivalry was growing between the expanded North West Company and the Hudson's Bay Company. Mackenzie knew that in whatever way possible, he had to increase the number of rich, lush beaver pelts he collected.

Pond's post was more comfortable than he had anticipated. Even fresh vegetables were in good supply. This was rare in the *pays d'en haut*. "On the banks of the Elk River, where he had remained for three years, he had formed as fine a kitchen garden as I ever saw in Canada," wrote Mackenzie.

On average, the voyageurs would paddle fifty strokes a minute and they could maintain that pace all day. But they would have to increase their strokes when traveling against the current.

During the daylight hours he and Pond tramped miles on snowshoes, meeting the Cree and the Chipewyan. They talked to them about their trading preferences and questioned them about water routes and trails that might lead westward. In the evenings they would sit by a warming log fire and study maps and journals by candlelight.

They discussed Captain James Cook's recent sailing adventures on the Pacific Coast. Pond told his protégé that Cook had explored a deep inlet which he believed was the estuary of a great river leading inland. Pond was convinced that he also knew this river, but from a different angle. He confided to Mackenzie that the previous summer he had found a river leading out of Great Slave Lake. He was certain that it led westward and that it was Cook's river.

Mackenzie developed a great respect for Peter Pond. His knowledge was not just gained from books and maps. He knew people everywhere on the continent, in many different walks of life. When he met someone new, he would learn everything he could about their particular field or expertise. The previous summer he'd met a man who had actually sailed with Cook. That man, Pond told Mackenzie, had seen vast numbers of sea otters on the West Coast. Pond knew that the Chinese paid a great deal for sea otter pelts, and trade to China would be much easier from the Pacific.

Pond was a great explorer but, like Mackenzie, he was first and foremost a trader. Both men were looking for easier routes and methods of transporting more furs to more markets. More furs meant more money.

Together they tried to work out how far away the

Pacific Coast might be. Pond thought the river he had found had a northward curve, but he believed it would turn westward beyond the Rocky Mountains. He thought the coast might only be six days from Great Slave Lake.

Mackenzie thought constantly about Pond's river. It became an obsession. One day he would find that river and he would follow it to the Pacific Ocean.

CHAPTER EIGHT
Fort Chipewyan

PETER POND left Lake Athabasca in the spring of 1788. By this time a push to the Pacific had become part of Mackenzie's master plan. But before he could undertake such a journey, he had to make sure that the Athabascan post would run smoothly in his absence.

First he would talk Roderick McKenzie into joining him at Lake Athabasca to act as manager. He knew no one could be trusted more than his cousin. Rory had been planning to retire from the fur trade. He had decided that life in the *pays d'en haut* was not for him. Rory was more of a scholar than an adventurer. He was looking forward to reading his books by a pleasant, crackling fire, preferably back in the old country. He disliked the isolation of the wilderness. He wanted to live in a big city like London, not venture farther still into the *pays d'en haut*.

It was a miracle that Rory changed his mind. But Alexander Mackenzie was a smooth talker and could be extremely persuasive. He probably just kept talking in a calm, quiet, logical manner until eventually he wore Rory down. Then he talked some more, until Rory was caught up in his excitement and enthusiasm. Finally, retirement plans were put aside. Rory could not deny that trade would increase considerably if they could discover a route to the West Coast.

Alexander decided he should relocate his main Athabascan post to a more central location. Roderick's first duty, therefore, was to oversee the construction of a new fort. Pond's old post had been on the Elk River. Now a site was chosen on the south side of Lake Athabasca. Mackenzie decided to call the new post, Fort Chipewyan. It was on the exact same latitude as Stornoway, his birthplace, but the similarity ended there.

The new fort was built on a rise of land at the tip of a peninsula, and it was surrounded by a picket palisade. No doubt there were also one or more two-storey log towers inside the palisade. "Portholes" in the towers were useful for observation even if they were never necessary for shooting.

It was highly unlikely that defense would be necessary, but it was still considered wise to build a secure post. Rival native trappers or competitors from the Hudson's Bay Company could cause problems.

The new Fort Chipewyan was not as large as Grand Portage, but there were several buildings within its walls, and it could accommodate up to one hundred people.

Each man at Fort Chip had his own job. The hardy *hommes du nord* who had brought Mackenzie to the region put aside their paddles when the rivers iced over. A few spent the snowy season repairing canoes or building new ones and making snowshoes. Others became trappers, catching and shooting food for the fort. They did not hunt beaver – beaver were considered the native

Fort Chipewyan was considered the most luxurious fort in the North. It even contained a library.

people's entitlement. Other men employed at the fort acted as interpreters, clerks, craftsmen and traders.

There were native women within the walls as well. They were responsible for growing and tending crops, fishing, gathering firewood and making clothes and footwear. When worn over rough ground, moccasins had to be replaced almost daily.

The new fort was at the hub of the trading area. A whole network of navigable lakes and rivers was within easy reach, and Mackenzie hoped that the native people to the north of the lake would find it accessible. The Hudson's Bay Company claimed a monopoly for most of the new territory where they were now trying to gain a foothold, but the North West Company had refused to recognize such a claim.

Everyone watched with wonder as the spacious, modern fort took shape. During the autumn of 1788, Mackenzie closed down a few of Pond's older, less productive outposts and sent expeditions out in search of new trade. News of Fort Chipewyan spread far and wide. Native people were invited to come and trade at the new post. When they came, gifts were exchanged and rum, food and tobacco were shared before business was done. Alexander Mackenzie made "doing business" worth everyone's while.

Mackenzie opened new outposts where wintering traders could gain even more business. Fort Chip was like a stone dropped into the middle of a pond, and word of the center spread like ripples in ever increasing circles, farther and farther into the wilderness.

Rory worked hard to complete construction of the fort before winter set in. He paid close attention to details to make it more comfortable. There were fireplaces and windows in most of the buildings. The rooms were painted to make them bright, and he even added a library. If he was going to stay in the desolate North, he would make his dwellings as luxurious and comfortable as possible. They moved in before Christmas.

Mackenzie was impressed by the Chipewyan people. He considered them "altogether the most peaceable tribe of Indians known in North America." He noted how they were less reserved at first meeting than were many other tribes. They were easy to communicate with and always happy to share information.

He admired their clothing: "In the winter it is composed of the skins of deer, and their fawns, and dressed as fine as any chamois leather in the hair. In the summer their apparel is the same, except that it is prepared without the hair." He found the women "more agreeable than the men," but noted that their gait was awkward "which proceeds from being accustomed nine months in the year, to travel on snowshoes and drag sledges of weight from two to four hundred pounds." He added that their snowshoes were "of very superior workmanship."

Fort Chipewyan became a popular stopping point. Traders enjoyed not only the company and the food, but also Rory's infamous library. The fort became known as the Emporium of the North. Roderick jokingly referred to it as the "Little Athens of the Arctic Regions."

Feeding large groups of people was not usually a problem. At this new lakeside location, fish were a plentiful and reliable food supply. The traders set out enormous nets every day. They even fished through the ice in winter and discovered that fish stayed fresh when frozen!

Mackenzie was content. He had his cousin to keep him company that winter and he felt reassured that Rory was capable of looking after the fort when he set off in the spring. He would soon be traveling into unknown territory, and he was filled with an unquenchable curiosity.

When Mackenzie told the North West Company shareholders his plans, they encouraged him. They longed for a navigable trade route to the Pacific Coast. They envied the Hudson's Bay Company's traders' convenient trading route to the shores of Hudson Bay. It was a far easier route than the long trek to Montreal. The young man they had sent off to Lake Athabasca was now twenty-four years old. He was proving himself a skilled, adaptable leader.

CHAPTER NINE
The Northern Ocean

THE EXPEDITION set off on June 3, 1789. It was a large group, thirteen people in four birchbark canoes: Mackenzie, four French-Canadian voyageurs (two with their wives), a German, a native guide named English Chief, two of his wives, and two native people who would act as interpreters and hunters. Mackenzie began to keep a journal. Not only did he record the expedition's progress, but he wrote at length about the territory he passed through and the people he met along the way.

Over the years English Chief had come to know many prominent explorers and fur traders, including Peter Pond. He had followed the Coppermine River to the Arctic and he had also been to Great Slave Lake. He knew the *pays d'en haut* well and he was respected by everyone. He knew how to cope safely in dangerous waters and all kinds of weather, and he knew how to find food even when it was scarce.

Knowing he would have to face such hardships ahead, Mackenzie pushed his party right from the first day. He had no wish to be caught far from Fort Chipewyan when winter returned, and that could be as early as the end of October. They rose each day long before dawn and paddled until four or five in the afternoon.

In spite of poor weather, they reached Great Slave Lake in a week. This huge lake was still filled with massive, terrifying sheets of ice. With caution the party worked their way through an open channel to an unused trading post. There they took shelter from the rain and the cold for two long weeks.

Rather than touch their stock of food, the men set out nets and caught fish until the nets were destroyed by the moving ice. Even when the ice cleared, the enormous sea-like lake was still frightening. The explorers battled ice, rain, fog, wind and rough water as they searched for Pond's river.

Here they encountered the Yellowknives, though Mackenzie referred to them in his journal as the Red Knives. Their name came from the copper they used to make knives and other implements. Mackenzie accepted guidance from a man who claimed he could lead them to the river. But it turned out he knew no more about the river than they did.

Even though the ice was still plentiful, thick clouds of mosquitoes soon descended. "The troublesome guests," as Mackenzie called them, got into their eyes, their mouths and their food. Their faces were swollen with bites, and the incessant buzzing kept them awake at night.

They knew they must be near Pond's river, but Mackenzie and his party explored a maze of dead ends searching for the right channel. Finally they felt the pull of a current. The force of the water must mean they were

near the mouth of a significant river. They were drawn
into a shallow channel, 10 miles (16 km) wide. Their
spirits lifted as the canoeing became easier. As the river
narrowed, they traveled swiftly with the current. They
used sails on their canoes much of the time.

Along the way Mackenzie's party hid caches of pemmican for the return trip, covering them with rocks so
that animals could not dig them up. The hunters shot
geese, swans, ducks and partridges. Many varieties of
berries were now ripe, but it took a lot of picking to sat-
isfy the appetites of such a large group.

Mackenzie was ecstatic when the snow-capped peaks
of the Rocky Mountains came into view. Then his heart
sank when suddenly the river turned northward. Day
after day, it ran parallel to the mountains.

He thought about the entrance to the large river that
Captain Cook had discovered on the Pacific Coast.
Until now he had felt certain that Pond's river and
Cook's river were one and the same. But now he had
traveled far past the latitude of Cook's discovery. His
hope faded quickly.

July came. They had been underway for a month.
Mackenzie had no idea where this river was taking them
or how much farther they would have to travel to its
mouth. The current grew stronger.

They met only small groups of native people. Most
had moved inland for summer hunting. The dwellings
along the shore were simple, "a few poles supported by
a fork, and forming a semicircle at the bottom, with
some branches or a piece of bark as a covering." Some
of the people they met had never encountered white
men. They rushed around in a fearful state when

Mackenzie's canoes approached, and sent women and children to hide in the forest.

Occasionally members of the tribes they met would travel with them as guides for a time, but once they reached a certain distance from home, they would desert. One of these guides was petrified when the voyageurs shot off their guns as a salute. He had never heard the sound of gunfire before.

English Chief, always the soft-spoken diplomat, could usually reassure the tribes they encountered and persuade them to accept small gifts such as beads, knives, flints or hatchets. Unlike the native people in the Athabascan region, people here had not yet been introduced to tobacco and liquor and showed little interest in them. On several occasions, Mackenzie left gifts for native people who had run away in fright.

The river narrowed and began to make eerie hissing sounds. The people of the area warned of dangerous rapids, so the explorers proceeded with extreme caution. They finally realized that a very strong current was the cause of the strange sounds.

Members of the Dogrib and Slave tribes told them that it took so long to follow the river to the sea that they would die of old age before they got there and back. They told fantastic tales of a land filled with monsters and evil spirits. They had no wish to guide Mackenzie's party any farther. They warned that the land was so bleak and barren, the men would die of starvation if they continued.

English Chief explained the reasons for these worries. The Dogrib and Slave were in constant conflict with the Eskimo and were fearful of them. Mackenzie had to encourage his men to carry on.

He sat up at night observing the movement of the sun. He could write in his journal almost all night long and he knew what this meant. "At half past twelve I called up one of the men to view a spectacle which he had never before seen," he wrote. "When, on seeing the sun so high, he thought it was a signal to embark, and began to call the rest of his companions who would scarcely be persuaded by me, that the sun had not descended nearer to the horizon." Then he added his worst fears: "Going further in this direction will not answer the purpose of which this voyage was intended. These Waters must empty themselves into the Northern Ocean."

Nevertheless, he could not turn around now. He would be expected to make a full report of this journey. Before returning to Fort Chipewyan he had to determine for certain where the river was carrying them.

Eventually the land became flat and the river split into many channels. They came to a wide expanse of water that they first took to be an enormous northern lake until they saw icebergs and then whales.

When the baggage on the shoreline was soaked by a rising tide, Mackenzie knew for certain. He had reached an ocean, but he had reached the wrong one.

They had traveled the 1020 miles (1700 km) from Great Slave Lake in only fourteen days, an amazing 72 miles (120 km) a day. This feat had been accomplished partly because of the skill of the paddlers and the way Mackenzie had pushed them. The current had helped, as had the high winds. But they were terribly disappointed.

"For some time past," wrote Mackenzie, "their spirits were animated by the expectation that another day

In his journal, Mackenzie described seeing whales and pursuing them by canoe. He wrote that "...it was a very fortunate circumstance that we failed in our attempt to overtake them, as a stroke from the tail of one of these enormous fish would have dashed the canoe to pieces."

would bring them to the Mer d'ouest." Instead they now stared sadly at the Mer du Nord.

Mackenzie reported that "even in our present situation they declared their readiness to follow me wherever I should be pleased to lead."

But on the homeward journey Mackenzie met with no encouragement. The men soon realized that once again their leader was on the lookout for concealed western rivers and someone who might guide them. They were anxious to be home before winter and to avoid the dangerous people who lived beyond the mountains to the west who, according to the local people, could kill you with their eyes alone. Mackenzie knew when he was beaten and eventually admitted in his journal that he was "very much fatigued with this fruitless journey."

Mackenzie's guides had to spend a lot of time hunting for enough food to feed thirteen people, but no one went hungry. On the homeward journey Mackenzie wrote,

> We had not touched any of our provision stores [pemmican, etc] for six days in which time we had consumed two reindeer, four swans, forty-five geese, and a considerable quantity of fish: ...I should really have thought it absolute gluttony in my people, if my own appetite had not increased in a similar proportion.

Snow and ice had already begun to block the lakes and rivers when they reached Fort Chipewyan on September 12. The return trip had taken 102 days. Mackenzie knew a transcontinental waterway must exist, but he had not found it – yet.

Along the banks of the northern river, Mackenzie had witnessed evidence of a number of different minerals. He observed "several lumps of iron ore." And a little farther on he "experienced a very sulphurous smell, and at length discovered that the whole bank was on fire and... the beach covered with coals." In another location he "...found pieces of petroleum, which bears a resemblance to yellow wax, but is more friable." The value of these minerals would only be realized years later. For Mackenzie, the river deserved the name he gave it, the River of Disappointment. Later, Arctic explorer Sir John Franklin renamed it the Mackenzie.

CHAPTER TEN
Leave of Absence

A T GRAND PORTAGE in the following summer of 1790, Mackenzie was granted another share in the North West Company. This was in recognition of his management of Fort Chipewyan and had nothing to do with his explorations and discoveries. It had proven a clever inducement to pay the "wintering partners" part of their salary in this way. As far as the shareholders were concerned, the Arctic journey had been a waste of time and money.

But with or without their approval Mackenzie was determined to try again. He sent his men on small exploratory trips to discover more about every waterway in the region.

En route back to Fort Chipewyan from Grand Portage, Mackenzie made a stop at Cumberland House. Two Hudson's Bay Company men were there also. Mackenzie enjoyed their conversation but was dismayed to learn of their company's growing interest in the West Coast. These two men were trying to calculate the distance from Lake Athabasca to the Pacific, and they seemed to have far more skill at such calculations than he did.

Mackenzie had been questioning his mapping techniques since returning from the Arctic. He knew he could lead someone back to his River of Disappointment, but he could not describe its exact geographic position.

He took a leave of absence and traveled to England. He spent a winter in London where he studied mapping, navigation and astronomy. He bought new equipment that would allow him to calculate the latitude and longitude of geographical positions.

While in the old country, he spent time with Roderick's father in London, but he lost little time being social. He had a mission, and he felt he had to get back to Canada as quickly as possible. He did not even visit Scotland to see his sisters, Sybilla and Margaret, whom he had not seen since he was a boy of twelve.

Mackenzie sailed back up the St. Lawrence to Montreal early the following spring of 1792. Then he made the long trek to Grand Portage and on to Fort Chipewyan.

Before leaving for England, Mackenzie had decided on a starting point for his route to the Pacific – the Peace River. His exploratory parties had now followed it far to the west. They were confident that if they continued further, the river would take them to, and possibly through, the mountains. Mackenzie was optimistic that its source could not be too far from the Pacific Coast.

During Alexander's absence, Roderick had sent a crew up the Peace River with instructions to build a fort at the western edge of familiar territory. This would save time

**The voyageurs were great storytellers and they loved to
outdo one another telling wild tales around the campfire.**

the following spring. It would be the jumping-off point
for the push to the Pacific. The new post, Fort Fork, was
at the junction of the Peace and Smoky Rivers.

The cousins had little time for a proper reunion.
Briefly they exchanged news and then Alexander had to
be on his way. Winter was already nipping at his heels
when he set off for Fort Fork on October 10, 1792. The
weather was cold and raw. Several inches of snow fell,
and Mackenzie was afraid that the river would freeze
before he reached his destination on November 1.

He was somewhat disappointed on his arrival. The two
men who had been sent ahead in the spring had been busy
"squaring timber for the erection of a house, and cutting
palisades to surround it." But Fort Fork was not yet built.

There were seventy members of the Beaver tribe living in the area, and they greeted Mackenzie's canoes with enthusiasm and a great volley of gunfire. "If we might judge from the quantity of the powder that was wasted on our arrival," Mackenzie commented, "they certainly had not been in want of ammunition, at least during the summer."

It was a strange winter. One day in December, Mackenzie was puzzled by an uncommonly warm wind. The snow melted, and water covered the ice on the lake. He was experiencing his first chinook. In January, the temperatures dropped drastically, but fortunately he had moved from his tent to his newly constructed house just before Christmas, and other houses were close to completion. "The weather now became very cold," said Mackenzie, "and it froze so hard in the night that my watch stopped; a circumstance that had never happened to this watch since my residence in the country." He was also amazed to discover that ax blades became as brittle as glass at such temperatures.

Outside the palisade walls life was not easy for people or animals. One night a hungry wolf ventured among the Beaver homes and was caught in the act of carrying away a small child.

Mackenzie was surprised to discover that the Beaver people near Fort Fork did not have the same knowledge of medicine and healing herbs that many other tribes had. He was frequently asked for medical assistance. Though he had never been trained in surgical skills, he bravely helped whenever he could and fortunately he was usually successful.

On one occasion he attended a man who had almost

LEAVE OF ABSENCE

shot off his hand in a hunting accident: "I formed a poultice of bark, stripped from the roots of the spruce-fir, which I applied to the wound, having first washed it with the juice of the bark." Later when it was clean, he made a salve of "Canadian balsam, wax and tallow dropped from a burning candle into water." The patient was soon hunting again. "When he left me," Mackenzie reported, "I received the warmest acknowledgments, both from himself, and the relations."

His method of curing a man of blood poisoning was somewhat more European: "...the pain was violent, and accompanied with chilliness and shivering. This was a case that appeared to be beyond my skill, but it was necessary to do something..." When his "volatile liniment of rum and soap" appeared to be of little help, he decided to bleed his patient, as was the custom of the day. "I ventured, from absolute necessity, to perform that operation for the first time... and in a short time he regained his former health and activity."

The native people he now traded with were mostly Beaver. Mackenzie was impressed by their skills. "These Indians are excellent hunters," he commented. But he was concerned about how hard they worked. "Their exercise in that capacity is so violent as to reduce them in general to a very meager appearance."

The Beaver had once been part of the Chipewyan nation, but Mackenzie felt they were more vicious and warlike than the Chipewyan he had known on Lake Athabasca. They were even brutal with one another on several occasions, fighting to the death with knives or guns.

During the winter months, the voyageurs constructed

a large canoe for their fast-approaching journey. It was 25 feet (7.5 m) long and could carry 2,992 pounds (1,360 kg). But the canoe had been built to Mackenzie's specifications and was so light that "two men could carry her on a good road three or four miles without resting." Their cargo would include gifts for the native people, arms, ammunition and baggage. Ten men would be aboard: Mackenzie; his lieutenant, Alexander Mackay; six voyageurs and two young Beaver men from the region of Fort Fork. They were to act as guides, hunters and interpreters. A dog would come, too, but he would not be permitted to ride in the canoe. He would run along the shore.

CHAPTER ELEVEN
Unknown Territory

MACKENZIE knelt with his men to pray, then he stepped into the water, and into the heavily laden canoe. It was not a happy send-off. A few of the men staying behind at Fort Fork were so fearful for the safety of their departing friends, that they wept on the shore as they mournfully called out their wishes for a bon voyage. Mackenzie breathed a sigh of relief when they were finally out of sight. Even so, his mind was racing. They would be traveling into unknown territory now. They had no idea what perils might lie ahead. No white man had ever crossed the Rocky Mountains.

Most of the voyageurs he knew well and trusted. But what of the two young Beaver guides? He had known them only a short time. Could he trust them? Would they stay with him? This time he had to reach the Pacific Ocean and he knew that his success would depend a great deal on the reliability of these guides.

Mackenzie admired the surrounding countryside. The weather was mild, and the trees along the shore were just coming into leaf. Elk grazed on the hills, and buffalo calves scampered beside their mothers on the plains. The surroundings were peaceful but, on the Peace River itself, the men had to paddle hard against a swift current.

The overloaded canoe began to leak almost immediately. The men had to unload and spread spruce gum on its weak spots. Mackenzie grew anxious. He paced along the shore, overseeing the repair work and urging the men to work quickly. They were losing precious time.

The explorers were barely underway again when Beaver hunters hailed them from the shore. The guides explained to Mackenzie that these people were their friends. Mackenzie knew they wanted to stop, but he would not. They had already lost enough time. He had to clench his teeth and work hard at remaining calm when his voyageurs, paying more attention to the

The voyageurs would often have to work late at night making repairs to their birchbark canoes.

hunters than to the river, ran the canoe onto a reef and the stop became a necessity. Much against Mackenzie's wishes, this was where they had to spend their first night.

The guides were delighted. It had been hard for them to part with their families and set off into the unknown. This delay meant one last chance to visit with people they knew. Mackenzie reluctantly gave them permission to go off for the night, afraid that he wouldn't see them again. Before they left, he solemnly reminded them how much he depended on their loyalty and how important they were to the success of the expedition.

This was their land and only they knew how to survive here. They were excellent at tracking, trapping and hunting. Possibly even more important, they were interpreters. Not only could they converse with the native people in this region, but in all likelihood they would understand the language of the next few tribes they met along the way.

Mackenzie was greatly relieved when the two Beaver guides returned at daybreak. One of them reported what his uncle had said to him:

> My nephew, your departure makes my heart painful. The white people may be said to rob us of you. They are about to conduct you into the midst of our enemies, and you may never more return to us. Were you not with the Chief, I know not what I should do, but he requires your attendance, and you must follow him.

On the journey many guides would join Mackenzie and then desert him, but these two Beaver men remained trustworthy and loyal.

The Beaver guides told Mackenzie that they believed the sea was about ten days' travel from the mountains.

Once they were in the mountains, the character of the river changed drastically. The first native people they met in this region were impressed that the men had traveled such a distance. They knew little of what lay beyond the mountains, but felt certain that it was impossible to get to the sea by canoe.

Mackenzie gazed up at the harsh, awe-inspiring peaks that surrounded him. They were higher than any he had ever seen. The snow on the mountain tops was melting and tumultuous waterfalls thundered down to the rising river.

The Peace now raced through steep, narrow canyons. The rapids were so dangerous they frequently had to tow the canoe. Mackenzie realized that one false step could mean losing everything. Loose rocks came crashing down from the sodden cliffs. Sharp, jagged fragments wore out their shoes and cut into their feet.

Portages became more and more frequent. One was 12 miles (19 km) long. Mackenzie made the decisions and supervised the men, but he also worked right alongside them, even helping to cut pathways with his ax.

One day the guides pointed out the enormous footprints of a grizzly bear and the deep, dark cave that was the bear's den. They explained that they would never attempt to kill such a bear except in a party of three or four.

There seemed to be no beginning or end to the mountains. They loomed overhead, their peaks lost in swirling cloud. At one point, Mackenzie's men had to cut steps in the rock face before they could continue.

Generally the guides took the lead, but here Mackenzie went first. He eased himself along the steps, then leaped down onto a small landing where he received each of the men on his shoulders.

On a few occasions Mackenzie went on with one of the guides to investigate what lay ahead of them. He would climb partway up a mountainside or an especially tall tree to get a view.

So driven was Mackenzie to complete his marathon journey, he rarely allowed himself time to dwell on discomfort or danger. He did, however, have empathy for his weary fellow travelers. He would boost their sagging spirits with praise and encouragement. He would raise their energy levels with a "kettle of wild rice sweetened with sugar." And there was always, of course, the reward of a ration of rum.

I had… the passions and fears of others to control and subdue. Today I had to assuage the rising discontents, and on the morrow to cheer the fainting spirits, of the people who accompanied me. The toil of our navigation was incessant, and oftentimes extreme; and in our progress over land we had no protection from the severity of the elements, and possessed no accommodations or conveniences but such as could be contained in the burden on our shoulders, which aggravated the toils of our march, and added to the wearisomeness of our way.

Eventually, the river became one white sheet of foaming water. They had to carry the canoe and all their equipment up one side of a mountain and down the other, clearing a path through dense forest as they went.

On the ascent they tied the canoe to a tree, then eased it up a bit and tied it to another. Progress was painfully slow. They stayed put for a day after this perilous portage. Mackenzie afforded his men this luxury partly because they truly needed a day of rest but also because of torrential rain. Mackenzie was more liberal than usual with the rum rations as they sat idly watching the river rush past them, and the men consumed a whole keg. He then amused himself by writing a letter about their hardships, enclosing it in the empty rum keg and sending it swirling off in the current.

On the last day of May, they came to a fork in the Peace. The voyageurs wanted to take the calm northern route. Mackenzie disagreed – an elderly native at Fort Chipewyan had warned him against the northern fork. Mackenzie got his way, but the southern route was difficult.

They often had to haul the canoe along the river's edge, clinging to branches so they wouldn't be swept away. Again and again they had to stop and make repairs.

A young Sekani drew Mackenzie a map of a river that flowed west to the great "Stinking Lake." Though he warned that the river was a dangerous one, Mackenzie's hopes were high. The Stinking Lake must be the Pacific Ocean, he thought.

The Sekani agreed to guide the men, and eventually they came to a short portage between two lakes. It looked like any other portage, but the guide explained that it was a place of great significance because it was the highest point they would reach on their journey. From now on they would be traveling with the current. The water would be flowing toward the Western Sea.

At this spot, native people had left old canoes and many smaller items in baskets hanging from the trees. According to custom, Mackenzie helped himself to a net, some hooks, a goat's horn and a wooden trap. He left in exchange a knife, some fire-steels, beads and an awl.

Despite the fact that their canoes now traveled with the current, the going did not become easier. Once when they were fighting treacherous rapids, and the two guides were walking to lighten the load, Mackenzie offered to walk as well.

"Oh, no," one of the voyageurs said jokingly. "If we're going to perish, let's all go together!"

So Mackenzie remained on board. He never expected his men to do something he would not do himself. Moments later the stern smashed against a rock. Then the canoe swung around and the bow struck the rock, too. Thrown into the rushing, freezing water, the men held tight to the flattened canoe.

The guides watched in horror from the shore, too overwhelmed to try to help. They sat down and wept while their comrades were tossed about like driftwood for several hundred yards.

They were all badly shaken by the time their feet finally touched bottom in a calm eddy. Mackenzie stayed in the freezing water holding onto the outside of the flattened canoe until he was sure everything that could be saved had been carried ashore. Numb with cold, bruised and exhausted, he too finally staggered to dry land.

The drenched men collapsed on shore, at first unable to speak. Then with trembling voices they began to talk of how they had nearly died in the treacherous water.

Their canoe was ruined and they'd lost their bullets. It was time to give up and go home. Mackenzie did not respond until everyone was dry, well fed and seated by the fire with a tote of rum.

Then, quietly, he spoke. Yes, he agreed, they were lucky to be alive. And they should be thankful. He said he could understand that a few of them might want to turn back. But how would they feel returning home without achieving their goal? He reminded them that they were *hommes du nord* noted for their courage and resolution. The lost bullets were not a problem, he reassured them. They still had gunpowder and could make more. And as for the damaged canoe, he had complete faith in their ability to restore it. Mackenzie's words boosted the men's morale and raised their spirits. They agreed to carry on. If he was willing to take the risks, so were they.

The gear, including 62 pounds (28 kg) of gunpowder, had been spread out on the beach to dry. One voyageur, deep in thought, paced with his pipe and carelessly stepped over the drying gunpowder. It didn't ignite, but Mackenzie did! This time there was no tea and sympathy. He told the man what an idiotic thing he had done. Mackenzie had managed to stay cool and calm throughout the harrowing afternoon, but he had reached his limit. Now he ranted on about how they could have been blown sky high. The unfortunate voyageur was sincerely apologetic for his carelessness.

"I need not add," Mackenzie wrote in his journal later that night, "one spark might have put a period to all my anxiety and ambition."

CHAPTER TWELVE
The Peace River

THEY MANAGED to repair their patchwork canoe with quantities of spruce gum and little bits of oiled cloth. And when they reached "the bad river" that the Sekani had told them about, it seemed reasonably peaceful at first. But unfortunately the Sekani guide then deserted. He had been far from enthusiastic about traveling on this river in the first place, and when he spotted the smoke of Carrier fires, he left without a word.

The Carrier nation extended over a large territory and included several different tribes. Over the miles there were often only small differences in their language. In this area they lived in large wooden houses close to the water's edge. Most ran away when the canoes approached, but one group shot arrows over it and made threatening gestures from the shore.

Since leaving the Peace, the two Beaver guides had understood very few of the native people encountered along the way, but the Carrier tongue was similar to their own. They spoke quietly to the Carrier, while Mackenzie, unarmed, tried to appear calm and walked along the shore toward them. A peaceful powwow resulted. While Mackenzie gave treats of sugar to the children, the interpreters learned as much as they could about what lay ahead.

The Carrier suggested the men would be wiser to travel overland to the sea. Not only was this river hazardous, but downstream they would meet the warlike Shuswap. They called the Shuswap "Atnah" which Mackenzie thought was the name of their tribe. But the word actually meant stranger or foreigner. The Shuswap had arms they had obtained from the West, from men like Mackenzie. They were not to be trusted and they would kill the men if the rapids didn't.

Concerned, cautious, but as determined as ever, Mackenzie carried on. His expedition was now reinforced with a few nervous Carrier guides. As predicted, the Shuswap people did appear ferocious with their bows and arrows at the ready. But with the help of his guides, Mackenzie managed to reassure them that his intentions were peaceful, and that they were simply passing by on their journey to the sea.

They spent the night with these men and learned more about the treacherous river. On a piece of bark, an old man drew a map of the river and the surrounding countryside. In some detail he spoke of the falls, rapids and carrying places.

Mackenzie had to hesitate, lost for words, when one native asked curiously, "What can be the reason that you are so particular and anxious in your inquiries of us respecting a knowledge of this country: do not you white men know everything in the world?"

Mackenzie replied that he and his men certainly were acquainted with the principal circumstances of every part of the world. And that he knew where he was and where the sea was but he did not exactly understand what obstacles might interrupt him in getting to it. "Thus," he explained in his journal, "I fortunately preserved the impression in their minds, of the superiority of white people over themselves."

It became apparent to Mackenzie that they had made a grave error and they would have to backtrack. Far back up the river they should have followed the overland trail as they had been advised earlier.

He called the men together to discuss their choices. He had actually made up his mind that they must turn back, but he wanted each man on the expedition to feel that he was involved in this decision.

As usual Mackenzie began by praising the men for their fortitude, patience and perseverance. Then he discussed their choices. They could follow the treacherous river route to the sea, but they now knew just how difficult this would be. Or they could travel overland as the Shuswap had suggested, though unfortunately this would mean backtracking. They had been told that the overland route would be faster. This was important as they had lost precious time and their provisions were now dangerously low.

He told the men that the final decision was theirs, but under no circumstances would he return home without reaching the Pacific.

"I could not reflect on the possibility of such a disappointment," he wrote in his journal, "but with sensations little short of agony."

His inclusion of the men worked; they were all of a like mind. But they were weary and depressed and now,

The voyageurs enjoyed the challenge of a fast-moving river but, on occasion, the rapids were more dangerous than they had bargained for.

in their ruined canoe, they had to backtrack 384 miles (640 km) up the fearful river to the overland trail.

Paddling back up the river, Mackenzie was aware of their hunched shoulders. He knew that reaching the Pacific was nowhere near as important to his men as it was to him. Their enthusiasm was fading fast. He was fatigued as well, but he was as steadfast as ever in his determination to reach his goal. It had become an obsession.

He pondered as his men paddled. Each day it became more and more apparent that he was not going to find a navigable route to the western ocean, but there were other reasons for this journey. He was discovering new trading territory, he was recording information about the flora and fauna and the various Indian tribes, and he would also record what lay beyond. He and others had explored west as far as the Peace River. Cook had explored along the coast – and now when he reached the ocean, he would be filling in the blank area on the map.

When the Carrier saw Mackenzie returning, they fled into the forest thinking he had come back to attack them. The two Carrier guides joined them. Mackenzie knew that these guides were essential. He could not manage the overland trail to the ocean without being shown the way.

To make matters worse, the voyageurs began to quarrel with one another. Mackenzie believed they were actually angry with him, but dared not express their anger except to each other.

They grumbled as they paddled. The canoe was in such poor condition, one man had to bail constantly to keep it afloat. To top off a particularly bad day, they hit a stump, causing irreparable damage. They were forced to land on a small island in the midst of a violent thunderstorm. "Our canoe was now become so crazy, that it was a matter of absolute necessity to construct another."

The following morning, somewhat reluctantly, the voyageurs started work on a new canoe. Finding enough bark of the right kind was difficult, and they had to use the gum from the old canoe. Their spirits lifted, however, as the canoe took shape – and then soared when the Carrier guides finally reappeared.

CHAPTER THIRTEEN
The Overland Trail

MACKENZIE and his men had only a short distance to travel in the new canoe. Then at the start of the overland journey, they hid it under a covering of branches in the forest. They would not need it until they returned.

The men set off on the overland trail carrying all their belongings. The voyageurs were used to long portages and each of them carried a 90-pound (41-kg) pack on his back. Unlike many of his contemporaries Mackenzie usually carried something on portages, and on this occasion both he and Mackay carried packs of 70 pounds (32 kg) each. Mackenzie wrote, "the inconvenience of the tube of my telescope swung across my shoulder, which was a troublesome addition to my burden." The guides reluctantly carried 45 pounds (20 kg) each. They had been hired to guide and to hunt and they were not pleased to be laden down!

Mackenzie and his men camped the first night with a group of native people who were just returning from the coast. When they displayed a spear they had purchased there from Europeans, the sea finally seemed closer.

Mackenzie was lulled to sleep by these travelers singing by the fire. The melodies were sweet and sad at the same time. "It had," wrote Mackenzie, "somewhat the air of church music."

Everyone they met on the overland trail was eager to trade. Many had never seen a white man, but they knew all about the goods they might acquire from them.

The trail grew more difficult when it rained. The men used thin sheets of lightweight oiled cloth as raingear. Most of the native people they now met were following a well-worn trading route, though some were camping and fishing in their summer camps. Some were afraid of Mackenzie and his party at first. But they soon lost their fears when they realized that they were not facing a war-like people. The native people were always willing to share food, even if all they had was dried fish. They offered advice and often accompanied the men for a time, showing them the way.

They traveled through a beautiful valley, then climbed high into snowcapped mountains. When they reached the summit, the guide pointed to a "stupendous" mountain and explained that between it and where they

The Grease Trail

Native people had traveled for hundreds of years along the route that Mackenzie followed overland to the sea. They used this trail for visiting and hunting but especially for trading. The route is often referred to as the Grease Trail because of the eulachon oil that was carried inland for trade. The oil from these small fish is still used in medicines and as a food preservative. The fish is eaten fresh, smoked or salted.

stood flowed a river that they could follow the last few miles to the sea.

Mackenzie noticed a change in the climate when they descended a steep precipice into another beautiful valley. Here summer was more advanced. The air was moist, the valley floor was covered with moss and the berries were already full and ripe.

After dark they came to a village where the native people displayed not the least bit of concern at so many men appearing before them so late at night. They graciously conducted Mackenzie into one of their houses.

> They made signs for me to go up to the large house, which was erected, on upright posts at some distance from the ground. A broad piece of timber with steps cut in it, led to the scaffolding even with the floor, and by this curious kind of ladder I entered the house at one end; and having passed three fires, at equal distances in the middle of the building, I was received by several people, sitting upon a very wide board, at the upper end of it.

He shook hands with the man he presumed to be the chief. Then he and his men were presented with a feast of roasted salmon, salmon roe, gooseberries and sorrel. Boards were prepared for the men to sleep on, and Mackenzie wrote that he had "never enjoyed a more sound and refreshing rest." He called the place Friendly Village.

The people at Friendly Village ate only fish. They believed that if the fish smelled meat, they would swim away and the villagers would die of starvation. They were so upset when one of Mackenzie's men threw a venison bone into the river, that they dove in, retrieved it and then burned it.

The villagers lent the group canoes and guides. As they proceeded on their journey, Mackenzie noted that the river was an unusual milky turquoise color, "the colour of asses' milk." On either side of the valley, the mountain ranges were topped with glaciers.

The inhabitants of the next village were not quite so friendly. They approached with spears, axes, bows and arrows. Mackenzie, acting as though nothing was unusual, shook hands with the nearest man, then with another and another. One elderly man hugged him, and then hugs were exchanged all around. They shared a delicacy made from the inner bark of the hemlock tree. Square cakes of bark had been soaked in water, pulled apart, and then sprinkled with salmon oil.

Communication was difficult. The guides did not speak a language anything like this one. Nevertheless, using sign language, the chief told them of his trip to the sea ten years earlier. He had seen two large ships carrying Europeans. Mackenzie realized these ships must have been Captain Cook's. And the chief's dugout was just like one Cook had described.

CHAPTER FOURTEEN
The Pacific Ocean

MACKENZIE and his men were surprisingly calm when they finally reached the Pacific. There were no loud shouts, cheers or backslaps. No hats were thrown in the air. As they looked down a long fiord toward the sea, they found the sight a little disappointing. They had hoped to see the open waters of the ocean, and so they decided to carry on. It was foggy and the steep mountains rising on both sides of the inlet were shrouded in cloud. Along the way they saw sea otters, porpoises, ducks, gulls and eagles.

Mackenzie took compass readings, but he was not able to make proper observations without the sun or the stars. These observations would be vital proof that he had reached his destination. It became windy, and they finally had to stop because their leaky canoe was taking on too much water in the high swell.

The next day they met three canoes carrying fifteen men. These native people were not at all like their peaceable neighbors of Friendly Village. Their leader was disagreeable and rude. He repeatedly informed Mackenzie that he had recently been fired at by white

Ocean Encounter

The native people Mackenzie encountered as he tried to reach the ocean were probably of the Bella Bella nation. They did have a somewhat ferocious reputation at that time in history.

In his journal Mackenzie says these people spoke of a large canoe that had appeared from the direction of the open sea only a few weeks earlier. And they mentioned two names again and again, "Macubah" and "Benzins." It seems quite likely that "Macubah" was Captain George Vancouver. "Benzins" may have been his botanist, Archibald Menzies. One of Vancouver's men may have unwisely fired over the heads of the Bella Bella when their behavior appeared threatening. Such an action, however, was not recorded in Vancouver's journal.

men who had come from the direction of the sea in a large canoe. He boldly entered Mackenzie's canoe, grabbing and examining its contents. He tried to force Mackenzie to come to his village. Vastly outnumbered, the explorers were in a perilous situation.

Mackenzie then noticed a beach where they could land, the only suitable landing place he'd spotted in some time. To the right of the beach and above a steep, rocky shoreline was a small clearing. It appeared to be the site of an old settlement, long deserted but strategically located for defense. By the time they had climbed to the clearing, ten canoes had gathered below.

When the native people again tried to convince Mackenzie to accompany them to their village, he admitted his concern to his men. He had accepted similar invitations all across the continent, but he was seriously apprehensive about this one.

The men attempted to trade with the native people because they had little food remaining and they had seen seal and fish in one of the canoes. Mackenzie offered a bolt of cloth, but the natives were only interested in items he dared not part with, such as his surveying instruments and his gun.

Although Mackenzie's party had little to eat – "Our whole daily allowance did not amount to what was sufficient for a single meal" – they lit a fire for warmth and reassurance. They prepared to defend themselves if they had to, but fortunately, when the sun set, the canoes slipped away.

The men watched in pairs through the long silent night and were thankful to be alive to greet the dawn. They wanted to be on their way immediately, but Mackenzie eyed the clear sky thankfully and set to work to take his readings.

He was busy with his instruments when the canoes began to return. Only one man came in the first canoe. He simply watched, silently, as Mackenzie worked.

Mackenzie's men glanced nervously at each other and toward the shore. Two more canoes had landed and several more, well manned, were fast approaching. Their guide from Friendly Village said these men were warlike and dangerous and he, too, urged them to make a quick departure.

Mackenzie blocked his ears to their anxious talk and worked on. He feared what might happen next. But incredibly, the native people simply gathered around him. They admired the unknown instruments and watched, fascinated, as Mackenzie completed his calculations.

One task remained. Mackenzie mixed vermilion with grease, producing a red paint-like mixture, and in large bold letters he wrote on the rock face: "Alexander Mackenzie, from Canada by land, the twenty-second of July, one thousand seven hundred and ninety-three."

Only then did he climb into the waiting canoe and turn his back on the Pacific.

On the return journey they traveled as quickly as possible. They were anxious to travel through the mountains and reach Fort Fork before the snow came.

They did make a stop at Friendly Village, however, where Mackenzie was once again warmly received. He now called the chief by his name, Soocomlick, and the two men exchanged gifts before they parted.

Mackenzie gave the chief two yards of blue cloth, an ax and several knives. Soocomlick presented his new friend with an exceptionally large oyster shell. These shells were of great value in the area and were used to make bracelets and earrings. The young chief also supplied the men with as much fish as they could carry. Mackenzie was fascinated by many of Soocomlick's articles and would have procured more, but he wanted to

Alexander Mackay

Alexander Mackenzie never returned to the Pacific Coast, but his lieutenant, Alexander Mackay did. Though he did not meet up with Soocomlick again, he was back on the West Coast in 1811 on John Jacob Astor's ship, the *Tonquin*. He explored the mouth of the Columbia – the river Mackenzie had hoped to explore. Then he traveled to the west coast of Vancouver Island, where he died attempting to defend the ship against a hostile tribe.

Mackenzie and his party had definitely reached salt water, but they were still far from the wide-open ocean, high waves and distant horizons that they had hoped to see.

keep their packs light for the homeward journey. The men of the village accompanied the travelers for about a mile before regretfully waving them on their way.

Mackenzie, weary to the bone, had no intention of ever returning, but he led Soocomlick to believe that he would be back and that he would come by sea on his next visit. The chief asked him to bring a gun and ammunition at that time, and he promised an abundance of sea otter skins in return.

Before setting off up the steep precipice, they had to cross a river. It was extremely fast moving and about 3

A Dog Came, Too

When Alexander Mackenzie crossed Canada, he traveled with a dog. "Our Dog" was never named, but he was a faithful worker and well loved by the men. He ran along the shore and through the forest most of the way, as there was no room for him in the canoe. Mackenzie mentions "Our Dog" again and again in his journal.

As he was a working dog, he helped find food and he acted as sentry for the men. Though he was never treated as a pet, the men grew increasingly fond of him during their long journey. They rescued him from a river when he was swept away by a current and trapped under driftwood. The men were sad and worried when he went missing — then ecstatic when he reappeared on their homeward journey. "We all felt the sensation of having found a lost friend," Mackenzie wrote in his journal.

feet (1 m) deep. One of the guides had not been well and was still quite weak. Mackenzie carried the young man across on his back.

Throughout the journey, the men helped one another without a thought of rank or class or color of skin. Later as they were nearing the Peace River, Mackenzie needed assistance. He had such severely swollen ankles he was unable to walk on one long portage. "I was obliged, though with great reluctance, to submit to be carried over it."

Fortunately, being later in the season, the rivers had gone down and were much less turbulent. But Mackenzie noted, "We found almost as much difficulty in carrying our canoe down the mountain as we had in getting it up."

The return journey was exhausting, and the men were bone tired. But now that they were on the way home, their spirits were good. For a time food was scarce, but then they found themselves once more "in the midst of abundance," dining like kings on a buffalo one day, a bear the next and then an elk.

They were delighted to be able to glide with the current on the Peace for the final miles of the journey. At the mouth of a small tributary, Mackenzie discovered four beaver pelts left on the shore. They had been promised to him by a native on the outward trip. He was so impressed with the man's honesty, he rewarded him with goods worth "three times the value of the skins."

CHAPTER FIFTEEN
Leaving the North

ON THE AFTERNOON of August 24, 1793, Alexander Mackenzie and his crew rounded the final bend on the Peace River and once again could see Fort Fork. They shot off their rifles, raised a flag and lifted their voices in song. On that last lap they paddled so furiously, the men at the fort didn't even have time for an answering volley! The trip home took only thirty-three days, less than half the time spent on the outward journey.

Mackenzie stayed briefly at Fort Fork and then carried on to Fort Chipewyan, where he was looking forward to spending the winter with his cousin. He was disappointed to discover that Roderick had been sent on to another post.

Mackenzie was understandably tired but also extremely depressed that winter. The long, difficult journey had been hard on his health. He would never completely regain his fitness and strength. His legs ached, his ankles were constantly swollen and he was exhausted.

He tried to organize and polish the many pages of

journal writings from his voyages, but he found he couldn't concentrate on the monumental task. "Dear Roderick," he wrote. "What a pretty situation I am in this winter – starving and alone – without the power of doing myself or any body else any service." He longed for his cousin's company. Rory was a true scholar and would have been a great help.

Dear Roderick: It is now the season I promised to write to you, and would wish I could fulfill another promise I made you last Fall and this Winter... my journal. I wished that you should peruse it at your leisure before any other person, as I expected you would examine the calculations, and correct the diction with that freedom which one friend might expect from another.

When he had left the North and was on his way to Montreal, Mackenzie stopped at Fort York (now Toronto) to call upon Lieutenant-Governor Simcoe.

He confided in Rory as he would have confided in no one else. Not only was he having aches and pains and trouble concentrating, but he also dared not close his eyes because he was having visions. He feared that he was near complete collapse. He knew he could take no more isolation and he must leave the North as soon as possible.

When spring came, Mackenzie left Fort Chipewyan for the last time. He met with his North West Company partners at Grand Portage for their annual meeting. They had little interest in hearing about his western sojourn, but announced that they required a man with

John Graves Simcoe's living accommodations astonished many of his guests. He and his family lived in a two-room tent and ate most of their meals outside.

his energy and boldness in Montreal. They needed someone to act as agent and intermediary between the inland traders and the Montreal organizers. As Mackenzie was ready for a change, this idea suited him.

En route east, he stopped at York, where he met with the first lieutenant-governor of Upper Canada, John Graves Simcoe. Lady Simcoe, who was a fervent diary keeper and most excited about the visit, wrote that Mackenzie had "brought the Gov. a Sea Otter Skin as a proof of his having reached that Coast. He says the Savages spear them from the Rocks... The Otter Skins are sold at a great price by those who trade on the coast to the Chinese."

Lady Simcoe was fascinated to learn about the customs of the coastal people:

> The Indians near the Coast live on fish which they are very dextrous in catching, they dry salmon in boxes in a kind of upper story in their Huts. They prepare the Roes beating them up with sorrel till it becomes a kind of caviar & when the salmon are dried, boil & mix them with oil. These savages never taste meat...

Hoping for a little more interest in his western discoveries, Mackenzie outlined to Simcoe the advantages of setting up trading posts on the Pacific Coast. Mackenzie spoke to the right person. Although the North West Company had not been too impressed by his discoveries, Simcoe was. He was quick to inform members of the British government of Mackenzie's discoveries and his ideas for western expansion of the fur trade.

In Montreal, Mackenzie became a powerful and

influential agent for the North West Company. He spoke at length of his plans and ideas for expansion of trade to the West Coast. Until that time trading had only been undertaken by visiting ships.

He also proved himself an excellent advocate for the interests of the wintering partners. They had feared Mackenzie's new importance would change him, but he had endured the hardships of life in the North and he understood their problems. He stood up for them and backed their demands for more shares and more influence in the organization of the company.

But despite fame and acclaim, the situation at company headquarters was not a happy one. Simon McTavish had always rankled Mackenzie, and their relationship was now worse than ever. The company was not supposed to be under the rule of one person, but somehow McTavish was managing to make all the decisions. Mackenzie was not the only one irritated by his tyrannical behavior. All the partners were.

Finally a number of the partners broke away and formed the "New North West Company." They marked their packs "XY" for easy identification and soon became known as the "XY Company."

In 1799 Mackenzie also left the North West Company. Roderick and William McGillivray begged him not to leave, but Mackenzie could stand the conflict no longer. He and Simon McTavish simply could not work together. Mackenzie also joined the XY Company.

CHAPTER SIXTEEN
England

IN 1799 MACKENZIE traveled to England. He had at last completed his journals and was anxious to find a publisher. His book came out in 1801 with the long title: *Voyages from Montreal on the River St. Laurence, through the Continent of North America to the Frozen and Pacific Oceans, in the Years 1789 and 1793.*

Though the events which compose my journals may have little in themselves to strike the imagination of those who love to be astonished, or to gratify the curiosity of such as are enamoured of romantic adventures; nevertheless, when it is considered that I explored those waters which had never before borne any other vessel than the canoe of the savage; and traversed those deserts where an European had never before presented himself to the eye of its swarthy Natives; when to these considerations are added the important objects which were pursued, with the dangers that were encountered, and the difficulties that were surmounted to attain them, this work will, I flatter myself, be found to excite an interest, and conciliate regard, in the minds of those who peruse it.

It was called a "travel book," and though that sort of reading was popular at the time, Mackenzie was nervous about presenting himself to the public as an author. "I am not a candidate for literary fame," he said. But the book was an immediate bestseller.

Mackenzie was knighted by King George III and suddenly he was in demand at fine dinner parties. A grand ball was given in his honor and he was often seen in the company of royalty.

Before returning to Canada, Sir Alexander met with his sisters for the first time in many years. By this time Sybilla and Margaret were both living in England.

Mackenzie was hailed as a hero on his return to Montreal. He was made head of the XY Company, now often referred to as Sir Alexander Mackenzie and Company.

Unfortunately the competition between this company and the North West Company had become vicious, involving bribery, blackmail, fighting and even bloodshed. When Simon McTavish died in 1804, however, peace was restored and the XY Company merged back into the North West Company.

Roderick must have been particularly happy. He had become a partner in the North West Company when Alexander had left, and his friendship with his cousin had been under a terrible strain.

At the time of the merger, the North West Company finally began to recognize Mackenzie's western discoveries and suggestions. "It requires only the countenance and support of the British Government," said Mackenzie in the final pages of his journal, "to increase in a very ample proportion this national advantage, and secure the trade of that country to its subjects."

James Finlay ascended the Peace to its junction and explored the northern fork rather than the southern fork traveled by Mackenzie. Then Simon Fraser began preparations for western trade and settlement. The ball began to roll. Mackenzie's vision of a cross-country chain of trading posts from coast to coast was becoming a reality.

Mackenzie also began serious negotiations for trade with China at this point. He made trips to New York City where he collaborated with the Americans in a scheme to trade furs from the Pacific Coast to China. Because there was still so little development in the western part of Canada, the scheme was only successful for a very brief time. There were simply not enough furs for both British and Asian trade.

Mackenzie was now leading quite a different sort of life. He lived in bachelors' accommodations in Montreal with William McGillivray. Handsome and smartly dressed, Mackenzie cut a dashing figure in the fashionable homes of Montreal. He worked hard for his company, but he also enjoyed an active social life.

Many mothers presented their daughters to the eligible bachelor. Mackenzie enjoyed the social whirl, but he decided it was time to settle down. He was in his forties now, and he wanted a family. He decided to retire completely from the fur trade, return to Scotland, find a country estate…and a wife.

The Beaver Club

The infamous Beaver Club was founded in Montreal in 1785. In order to belong, a man had to have spent at least one winter in the *pays d'en haut*. Alexander Mackenzie was a popular and enthusiastic member.

There were just nineteen members when the club was first formed. Each man wore a gold medal on a blue ribbon around his neck (below).

Most of these boisterous, free-spirited men had not found it easy returning to civilization after years in outlying fur-trading posts. At club meetings they shared their frustrations.

Dinner meetings began at four in the afternoon, and though

On one side of the medal was a picture of voyageurs in a canoe. Around the edges the name of the member was engraved along with the date of the first year he had spent in the *pays d'en haut*, and the Beaver Club motto, "Fortitude in Distress." On the other side was a beaver and the words "industry" and "perseverance" and the year 1785.

the married men left at midnight, bachelors like Mackenzie often stayed on until four in the morning!

The menu included such delicacies as roast beaver tails, sturgeon, venison steaks, pickled buffalo tongues, wild rice, a little pemmican for old time's sake and perhaps even moose muffle, which was made from the lips of a moose. And, of course, there were vast amounts of wine.

The highlight of the evening was the ceremonial "Grand Voyage." Each man grabbed a walking stick, a poker or a sword to use as a paddle. Then they seated themselves on the floor, where they paddled an imaginary canoe.

The North West Company storehouse in Montreal.

CHAPTER SEVENTEEN
Scotland

VERY SHORTLY after his return to his homeland, Alexander Mackenzie met Geddes Margaret Mackenzie. She was of the same clan but not a blood relation. Family records show that she was born in 1799, which meant she was only thirteen when she married fifty-year-old Mackenzie.

Mackenzie did not return to Lewis. The climate was far more temperate on the east coast of Scotland where Geddes had grown up. From her family, he purchased the estate of Avoch on the Moray Firth. They spent a good part of each year at Avoch but they also had a house in London where they went each winter.

Mackenzie was no longer involved in the fur trade, but he did keep up with what was going on in the business, and he was quick to voice his opinions. He feared, for example, that colonization would ruin the fur trade. He was strongly against the British government's plans to establish a settlement along the Red River (in what is now Manitoba) and he did all he could to dissuade the emigrants from signing up. He also felt strongly that the North West Company and the Hudson's Bay Company should join forces. "And then," he stated, "the trade might be carried on with a very superior degree of advantage..." This did come to pass, but not until just after his death.

Sir Alexander Mackenzie was content with his new, gentler life and he enjoyed his children – two sons and a daughter. He was proud of his estate high on the hill above the Moray Firth and worked hard to improve his property. He was also active in the nearby village and enjoyed chatting and visiting with the local deep-sea fishermen. He became involved in many local land improvement projects such as the building of a seawall between Avoch and the village of Fortrose.

Unfortunately these years of contentment did not last long. He wrote Roderick in January, 1817: "I have at last been overtaken with the consequences of my sufferings in the North-West...The symptoms of the disorder are very disagreeable and most uncomfortable. The exercise of walking, particularly up hill, brings on a headache, stupor or dead pain, which at once pervades the whole frame, attended with listlessness and apathy which I cannot well describe."

The following year, traveling home to Avoch with his wife and children after a visit to Edinburgh, he became critically ill. They stopped to rest at an inn, but he did not survive the night. Sir Alexander Mackenzie was fifty-six years old when he died in 1820.

Epilogue

MACKENZIE was the first European to cross North America by land. His journals were widely read. They were translated into French and German, and summaries were even published in Russian.

In the United States, President Thomas Jefferson acquired a first edition and read it with great interest. The final chapter discussed boundaries. Mackenzie had seen the three oceans that would mark Canada's east, north and west boundaries, and he proposed the line that should form the country's fourth boundary to the south.

With just a few exceptions our present U.S. – Canada border is much as Mackenzie proposed. But he did say, "the line must be continued West, till it terminates in the Pacific Ocean, to the South of the Columbia River." And had that suggestion been followed, Washington State would now be a part of the province of British Columbia.

Mackenzie's words no doubt influenced President Jefferson to make plans for two men, Meriwether Lewis and William Clark, to undertake a similar expedition below the border in 1805. A new American edition of Mackenzie's journal had been published by this time. It was smaller and more portable and of course it contained much useful information for the travelers. Jefferson presented it to Lewis and Clark, who carried it with them on their well-publicized expedition.

Mackenzie's geographic discoveries led to the expansion of the fur trade in the Northwest. Small fur-trading posts eventually became villages, and western settlement began. Railways and highways followed, to create a Canada that stretched from sea to sea.

But with greater settlement and a greatly expanded fur trade, the beaver began to disappear. An elderly native said to explorer David Thompson in the early nineteenth century, "We are now killing the Beaver without any labor, we are now rich, but shall soon be poor, for when the Beaver are destroyed we have nothing to depend on to purchase what we want for our families. Strangers now overrun our country with their iron traps, and we, and they will soon be poor."

Perhaps fortunately for the beaver, a new style of hat came into vogue in Europe. It was made of lacquered silk, very stylish, lightweight and less expensive. The race for beaver pelts was over.

But the years that followed were still fraught with misunderstanding. Canada's First Nations often refer to Mackenzie and his voyageurs as the country's first white tourists. That small group of men did little harm, really, except perhaps for the graffiti on the rock; but their visit was just the tip of the iceberg.

Misery followed in Mackenzie's wake. The early bickering between the North West Company and the Hudson's Bay Company led to violent battling. Over the years the native people had often worked closely with the white traders. A trust had grown... but when they witnessed the deceit, the extravagance and the brutal competition, they lost any respect that had developed.

But worse problems were to follow. As more and more settlers entered the country, diseases such as smallpox were introduced. The native people had no natural immunity and entire nations were wiped out. Mackenzie considered smallpox to be "the greatest calamity that could have befallen the Natives... small pox, which spread its destructive and desolating power, as the fire consumes the dry grass of the field. The fatal infection spread around with a baneful rapidity which no flight could escape, and with a fatal effect that nothing could resist."

By the end of the 1800s, Mackenzie's journals were out of print. Few people ever thought of the faraway rock on the Pacific Coast, and the explorer's graffiti was fading fast.

Then, in the 1920s, an effort was made to find the rock again. It wasn't easy. Using the calculations from Mackenzie's journals and taking certain variations into account, surveyors were finally successful. Although the original inscription had faded away, they had Mackenzie's words carved into the rock and filled with red cement. A monument was placed in the clearing above the rock.

*   *   *

On July 22, 1993, five hereditary chiefs and their families, all in ceremonial robes and headdresses, stood on the clearing above Mackenzie Rock ready to welcome their guests.

Mackenzie and the voyageurs were in fact students from Lakehead University who had spent three summers paddling and hiking across Canada to arrive at this exact spot at this precise moment.

Mackenzie Rock was still untouched by civilization. Dark forests covered the high, steep mountains from their cloud-covered tops down to the rocky shoreline, just as they had two hundred years before.

On cue, the costumed students arrived with whoops and hollers, weaving their way to the pebble beach through an audience of fifty boats. They were greeted warmly by the chiefs.

"You are a welcome sight," said Chief Siwallace. "While you are here, you will be living in peace with us."

Every word spoken was positive. Mackenzie's accomplishments were warmly acknowledged, but everyone stressed that Mackenzie would never have reached the Pacific Ocean without the assistance of the First Nations people.

In closing, everyone joined together and sang "O Canada." Then once again that magical, mystical spot was left in silence.

Glossary

Apprentice: A person who learns a trade by working with someone skilled in that trade.

Bourgeois: In the fur trade the "bourgeois" were considered men of higher social standing than voyageurs or farm hands. Bourgeois owned property or were engaged in business as owners or partners.

Cache: A hiding place for equipment or supplies; those things hidden in a cache.

Chamois: A soft pliable leather used for making clothing or for cleaning and polishing.

Chinook: A warm, dry wind that blows from the west over the Rocky Mountains, causing a sharp rise in temperature.

Dugout: A boat made from a hollowed-out log.

Eskimo: Inuit.

Gaol: Jail.

Gunnels/Gunwales: The upper edge of a canoe (or other boat) that forms a ledge around the whole vessel.

Jetty: A landing pier, wharf.

Latitude: Imaginary lines that run east-west around the earth's surface. Latitude is measured in degrees north or south of the equator.

Longitude: Imaginary lines running north-south on the earth's surface between the North Pole and the South Pole. Longitude is measured in degrees east or west of a standard line drawn through Greenwich, England.

Métis: The offspring of a native person and a white person, especially one of French ancestry.

Nor'Wester: A North West Company agent, wintering partner or employee.

Palisade: A fence made of tall wooden stakes planted in the ground, usually built for defensive purposes.

Pays d'en haut: The forests and plains stretching north and west beyond the Great Lakes.

Pelt: The untanned hide or skin of an animal.

Pemmican: Dry cooked meat pounded to a paste and mixed with fat. Since it kept indefinitely, pemmican was a staple food for the voyageurs.

Portage: A place where boats or canoes have to be carried over land from one body of water to the next.

Powwow: A meeting or conference among North American native people. Sometimes a celebration or ceremony before a hunt, battle or some other special event.

Spruce gum: A sticky, glue-like substance found in spruce trees that hardens when exposed to air.

Staves: The thin, narrow pieces of wood that form the sides of the canoe.

Stockade: A tall fence or enclosure often made of wooden posts driven into the ground side by side to keep out enemies or intruders.

Venison: Deer meat.

Vermilion: A bright red dye.

Voyageur: A person who worked in the fur trade and traveled mostly by canoe.

FOR FURTHER READING

Non-fiction

Bial, Raymond. *The Haida* (Lifeways Series). New York: Benchmark Books, 2001.

Bial, Raymond. *The Iroquois* (Lifeways Series). New York: Benchmark Books, 1999.

Campbell, Marjorie Wilkins. *The Nor'Westers: The Fight for the Fur Trade.* Toronto: Fitzhenry & Whiteside, 2002.

Dene Cultural Institute. *Dehcho: Mom, we've been discovered!* Yellowknife: Dene Cultural Institute, 1989.

Hacker, Carlotta. *The Kids Book of Canadian History.* Toronto: Kids Can Press, 2002.

Hayes, Derek. *First Crossing: Alexander Mackenzie, his Expedition across North America, and the Opening of the Continent.* Vancouver/Toronto: Douglas & McIntyre, 2001. (For older readers)

Hehner, Barbara, ed. *The Spirit of Canada.* Toronto: Malcolm Lester Books, 1999.

Huck, Barbara. *Exploring the Fur Trade Routes of North America.* Winnipeg: Hartland Associates, 2002.

Lunn, Janet and Moore, Christopher. *The Story of Canada.* Toronto: Key Porter Books, 2000.

Mercredi, Morningstar. *Fort Chipewyan Homecoming: A Journey to Native Canada.* Minneapolis: Lerner Publications Company, 1997.

Owens, Ann-Maureen and Yealland, Jane. *Forts of Canada.* Toronto: Kids Can Press, 1996.

Reed, Kevin. *Aboriginal People: Building for the Future.* Toronto: Oxford University Press, 1999.

Historical Fiction

Downie, Mary Alice. *Bright Paddles*. Toronto: Fitzhenry & Whiteside, 1999.

Harris, Christie. *Raven's Cry*. Vancouver/Toronto: Douglas & McIntyre, 1992. (For older readers)

Manson, Ainslie. *A Dog Came Too*. Groundwood Books, Toronto/ Vancouver, 1992.

More about the First Nations people and early explorers on the World Wide Web:

http://www.bcarchives.gov.bc.ca/exhibits/timemach/index.htm
British Columbia Archives presents the Amazing Time Machine.

http://www.canadiana.org/hbc
Written for 9- to 13-year-olds and including teacher resources, this site traces the history of the fur trade, the Hudson's Bay Company and more.

http://www.civilization.ca/indexe.asp
More on the First Nations and Canadian history, with special information for kids and teachers.

http://www.carlton.paschools.pa.sk.ca/pa/Canoeing/alexander_mackenzie.htm
Excerpts from Alexander Mackenzie's Journal (1801).

http://www.nativetech.org/
Native technologies. An educational web site emphasizing the Eastern Woodlands region, with sections on Beadwork, Birds and Feathers, Clay and Pottery, Leather and Clothes, etc.

http://www.canoemuseum.net/
The Canadian Canoe Museum, Peterborough, Ontario. How the canoe played a vital role in the development of Canada.

Index

118

Picture Credits

Pages 6-7 Map from *Voyages from Montreal on the River St. Laurence through the Continent of North America to the Frozen and Pacific Oceans in the Years 1789 and 1793* by Alexander Mackenzie; 10 National Archives of Canada/C2146; 17 Artist: Henry Popple, Engraver: W.H. Toms, *New York from the East, The Popple View*, 1733, Museum of the City of New York, The J. Clarence Davies Collection, 29.100.1520; 18 C.W. Jefferys/ National Archives of Canada/C73449; 22 Robert Auchmuty Sproule, William Satchwell Leney/National Archives of Canada/C41001; 24 C.W. Jefferys/National Archives of Canada/C73431; 25 National Archives of Canada/C17338; 28 Frances Anne Hopkins/National Archives of Canada/C2773; 31 (top) A.A. Chesterfield/National Archives of Canada/C69184 (bottom) William Armstrong/National Archives of Canada/C19041; 36 Joseph Bouchette/National Archives of Canada/C18834; 41 National Archives of Canada/C748; 44 National Archives of Canada/C79641; 49 Frances Anne Hopkins/National Archives of Canada/C2771; 54 Harry S. Watson/National Archives of Canada/C15244; 63 C.W. Jefferys/National Archives of Canada/C70230; 67 National Archives of Canada/C16415; 72 Frances Anne Hopkins/National Archives of Canada/C2772; 82 C.W. Jefferys/National Archives of Canada/C70270; 93 C.W. Jefferys/National Archives of Canada/C73712; 97 Sempronius Stretton/National Archives of Canada/C14905; 98 C.W. Jefferys/National Archives of Canada/C73667; 104 National Archives of Canada/C30782 (left) C30780 (right); 105 National Archives of Canada/C29925.

Acknowledgments

The following people have made my Mackenzie research stimulating and enjoyable: Friends and associates in the Alexander Mackenzie Voyageur Route Association; Joyce and David Dorsey, who organized a horseback ride along the overland portion of Mackenzie's trail; Rene Morton, a font of knowledge at the end of the trail in Bella Coola; Jim Smithers, who led the Lakehead University students during the three years of the Mackenzie bicentennial reenactment and his student voyageurs, who even let me ride in their *canot de maître*; Finlay MacLeod on the Isle of Lewis, who introduced me to Stornaway and showed me Melbost Farm; Gregor MacIntosh of Avoch, who showed me the house where Mackenzie lived in his retirement and his gravesite at the Avoch Parish Church.

I have referred to many books in my research but the book that made it all possible was Mackenzie's own journal, *"Voyages from Montreal on the River St. Laurence through the Continent of North America to the Frozen and Pacific Oceans in the Years 1789 and 1793."* It is probably the best adventure story ever written and should be required reading for every Canadian!